LEADING MASONIC ORGANIZATIONS

LEADING MASONIC ORGANIZATIONS

To Build and Sustain the York Rite of Freemasonry

Dr. Ashley Moye, 33⁰

Tampa, Florida

The views and opinions expressed in this book are solely those of the author and do not reflect the views or opinions of Gatekeeper Press. Gatekeeper Press is not to be held responsible for and expressly disclaims responsibility for the content herein.

LEADING MASONIC ORGANIZATIONS:
To Build and Sustain the York Rite of Freemasonry

Published by Gatekeeper Press
7853 Gunn Hwy., Suite 209
Tampa, FL 33626
www.GatekeeperPress.com

Copyright © 2023 by Ashley Moye

All rights reserved. Neither this book, nor any parts within it may be sold or reproduced in any form or by any electronic or mechanical means, including information storage and retrieval systems, without permission in writing from the author. The only exception is by a reviewer, who may quote short excerpts in a review.

Library of Congress Control Number: 2023930561

ISBN (paperback): 9781662936500

eISBN: 9781662936517

To Build and Sustain the York Rite of Freemasonry
Dr. Ashley Moye, 33°

Dedication

Alvin B. Amos Lodge #645, Texas, PHA
Warfield Lodge #44, Tennessee, PHA
Thomas A. Simms Lodge #170, Kentucky, PHA
Widow's Sons #202, Oklahoma, PHA
Mount Olive Lodge #3, Kansas, PHA
Golden Link Lodge #205, North Carolina, PHA
Hallie Selassie Lodge #90, Washington, PHA
Howard Z. Plummer Lodge #131, Maryland, PHA
George Washington Lodge #585, Grand Orient of Italy
Zillah Military Lodge #167, Oklahoma, PHA
Ester's Grace Chapter #170, Oklahoma, PHA
Terry A. Harris Guild #7, Oklahoma, PHA
Wallace W. Washington Chapter #46, Oklahoma, PHA
Michael A. Johnson Council #12, Oklahoma, PHA
Clifton B. Riley Commandery #18, Oklahoma, PHA
District 8 and District 12 Oklahoma, PHA
(Lodges, Chapters, Councils and Commanderys, DDGMs, DDGHP, DDGEC)

Contents

Introduction — 1

The Interdependence of the York Rite — 5

Common Pitfalls and Leadership Challenges — 7

A Chapter of Holy Royal Arch Masons — 33

A Council of Royal Select Masons — 55

A Commandery of Knights Templar — 75

To Sustain the York Rite — 87

Introduction

IF WE ARE ABOUT the business of Freemasonry, living its teachings and perpetuating the same, then the best of us shall always prevail. We commit ourselves to a lot of counterproductive customs and practices, yielding adverse outcomes. Too many of us continue to misrepresent and pervert what was intended for Freemasonry. We ascend to positions and ingratiate ourselves to merely exist in the moment. Too many of us in positions of leadership and influence are no longer fit to advance the greater ideas of the Freemasonry, nor fit for what these times demand of us. These problems exist in every type of organization in Freemasonry. It is fortunate that time ushers our usual practices into obsolescence, but we do well at ignoring our problems. Too many of us are afraid to speak up, but we must have the tough conversations and be mature men about working through our differences. For the sake of our future. Not for the good of an individual, but for the good of the Order.

Freemasonry is a fraternity. The York Rite of Freemasonry is particularly different from all the other rites. The make-up of the York Rite is four components: the Lodge, the Chapter, the Council, and the Commandery. The York Rite formation is a cascade of interdependence across the four organizations that presents several levels of complexity when it comes to managing the organizations as a whole. The Lodge as the foundation accepts petitions from any qualified man with or without prior masonic association. The Chapter only accepts petitioners who are Master Masons from the Lodge and in good standing. The Council only accepts petitioners who are both Master Masons from a Lodge and Holy Royal Arch Masons from a Chapter and in good standing. The Commandery only accepts petitioners who are both Master Masons from a Lodge, Holy Royal Arch Masons from a Chapter, and Royal Select Master Masons from a Council and in good standing.

The success of the York Rite requires that the organizations operate as one. That means the organizations within the York Rite must function in unison as one organization. One separate organization cannot survive without the other. Too often each organization operates exclusively, to its detriment, and presents leadership challenges across the York Rite. This begins with conflicts of time, money, and the overall satisfaction of a Brother's membership experience. Then Brothers have to choose to participate in one or two organizations or not participate at all. This is further compounded by a lack of alignment across the leadership of each organization. The result is the inability to grow and retain the membership needed to establish or sustain the York Rite as the whole of a single organization and body.

This book is a reflection of twenty years of lived and shared experiences as a Prince Hall–Affiliated Freemason. This book is not a deep dive into the history, philosophy, or ritualistic works of the York Rite of Freemasonry. This book provides suggestions for deliberate and practical approaches to establish, grow, and sustain the whole of the York Rite for the good of the Order and with the future in mind. It provides some alternative ideas and several tips in this regard:

- Understanding the interdependence of the York Rite
- Avoiding common pitfalls and leadership challenges
- Making membership affordable
- Providing a worthwhile membership experience
- Understanding the economic power of the organization

- Understanding the health of the organization with growth and retention rates
  - Understanding the need for leadership alignment
  - Establishing a positive community presence and identity

To the end of sustained economic power and positive social and economic change for our communities, the book is for organizations with established York Rites and those who desire to establish them.

The Interdependence of the York Rite

THE ANCIENT CRAFT LODGE, the Holy Royal Arch Chapter, the Royal Select Council, and the Knights Templar Commandery together form the York Rite of Freemasonry.

The Ancient Craft Lodge. The Lodge is the foundational organization of Freemasonry, which all other organizations depend on for qualified membership. At the Lodge, any qualified man might be accepted into Freemasonry and receive the first three symbolic degrees (1st—Entered Apprentice, 2nd—Fellowcraft, and 3rd—Master Mason).

The Holy Royal Arch Chapter. The Chapter is the second component of the York Rite. The Chapter depends upon the Lodge population from which it draws its membership. At the Chapter, any qualified Brother who is a Master Mason in good standing may petition to receive the four degrees of the Holy Royal Arch (4th—Mark Master, 5th—Past Master(virtual), 6th—Most Excellent Master Mason, and 7th—Royal Arch).

The Royal Select Council. The Council is the third component of the York Rite. The Council depends upon the Lodge and the Chapter's population from which it draws its membership. At the Council, any qualified Brother who is both a Master Mason and Holy Royal Arch Mason in good standing may petition to receive the three degrees of the Royal Select Master (8th—Royal Master, 9th—Select Master, and 10th—Super Excellent Master).

The Knights Templar Commandery. The Commandery is the fourth and final component of the York Rite. The Commandery depends upon the

Lodge, Chapter, and Council's population from which it draws its membership. A Brother has to be a member of all three. At the Commandery, any qualified Brother who is all three is a Master Mason, Holy Royal Arch Mason, and Royal Select Master Mason in good standing may petition to receive the three degrees of the Knights Templar (11th—Knight of the Red Cross, 12th—Knights Templar, and 13th—Knight of Malta).

The health and presence of the Lodge population are what dictate the viability of establishing and the capability of sustaining the York Rite. It is necessary that leaders be deliberate in reviewing and assessing the health of Lodges from time to time if there is a desire to establish the York Rite. The interdependence and complexity across the York Rite require establishment with sustainment in mind and leadership alignment and reciprocation at all levels.

Common Pitfalls and Leadership Challenges

WHAT IS THE AVERAGE life span of a Lodge, Chapter, Council, or Commandery? How often are Lodges, Chapters, Councils, or Commanderys closing? Our York Rites fail because of a lack of alignment, cooperation, and shared interests and responsibilities across the leaders of each organization. Though these things are required to realize success, this is easier said than done. Let's consider how a pitfall or challenge at one level might affect establishing and sustaining the entire body of the York. Since the foundation of the York Rite begins at the Lodge, it is logical to start here, through the lens of the Lodge.

Common pitfalls of Freemasonry include misrepresentation and perversion, membership affordability, and a negative membership experience. This encompasses the community-facing activities of the Lodge and other organizations in how Freemasonry is represented or perceived, and the member-facing activities of the Lodge in how satisfied a Brother is with his membership experience. If there is a desire to establish a York Rite or if there exists a York Rite body, then the leaders of the Lodge must operate the Lodge with the rest of the York Rite in mind.

Misrepresentation is the leading, most damaging threat and the biggest problem for our fraternity. Misrepresentation is *a false or misleading representation of something* and perversion as *to distort or corrupt the original meaning of something than what was originally intended.* Misrepresentation and perversion are the main reasons our communities have developed an often negative and undesirable perception of Freemasons.

We are in a fast-moving information and social age, and the way issues about Freemasons are greatly sensationalized, this can make recruitment and growth very challenging. We have all heard some undesirable things and have been asked some rather strange things about Freemasonry. In one regard, we feel the need to defend the truth of what we represent as a fraternity; in another regard, we have to accept the fact that Brothers continue to misrepresent and pervert the principal ideals on which our fraternity was built. We have to own that somewhere, someone has had a particular experience with Freemasons, which validates their preconceived ideas brought on by sensationalism, and feels the need to speak their truth about it.

There is a necessity to maintain secrecy, and some would say, privacy, but there is no longer a need for shadow operations anymore. The Lodge needs to change its approach and mindset on this because it is counterproductive. The Lodge has to first help to address misrepresentation and perversion at its level. This is notwithstanding the presence and activities of bogus or clandestine organizations which we know exist. It must address misrepresentation and perversion in membership development and training. Second, the good of the Lodge needs to be seen, and the community needs to see and realize the social and economic impact of the Lodge. The Lodge needs to actively publicize its service and impact on its communities. Last, the Lodge needs not to entertain conspiracy theorists, as we have a more important responsibility to represent our founding principles and ideas for the good of the Order.

A man will have his reasons for petitioning the Lodge. These reasons are often preceded by skepticism and doubt. Beyond the hype surrounding things like misrepresentation and perversion, a man often arrives at our fraternity through the personal relationships of family members or professional relationships among friends. This creates a unique personal understanding and expectation of what is to come once he is a member. The expected conflicts with the actual membership experience are another place where the Lodge will find challenges with member growth and retention. Stories of misrepresentation and perversion may have preceded a Brother's decision to join, and it is particularly disheartening for a Brother to subsequently experience it. Add in a lack of leadership direction, fraternal politics, and the whole of what makes for a negative membership experience. It is hard to retain Brothers who become dissatisfied with their membership experience. A Brother comes in and realizes no sense of belonging or direction and witnesses a lack of harmony or sense of brotherhood among men, while also being subjected to a growing number of counterproductive customs and practices.

There needs to be more attention given to the development and well-being of our membership in order to keep their interests. The Lodge first needs training and education programs, which include member and leadership development. Membership education includes, but is not limited to, member expectations, roles, rights, and privileges; history of the fraternity; and organizational operations, programs, and protocols. Leadership-based education includes subject matter related to managing organizations, particularly fraternal organizations. This is especially true where Brothers are elected and ill-prepared to be responsible for the Lodge. Second, the Lodge should take care in how it conducts the business of the organization, using sound business practices and judgment, getting rid of counterproductive customs. Brothers are often untrained, and we fail to get them involved in the work of the organization through things like committee assignments. We fail to keep Brothers informed of organizational activities and miss opportunities to conduct activities that promote brotherhood. We often don't make matters of organizational operations predictable to shape expectations and to ensure Brothers have time to properly plan and meet other obligations.

Membership affordability in terms of both time and money is the greatest of all conflicts with growth and retention. This matter of affordability from the standpoint of money is something we may all carry differing perspectives on, but the point here is regarding it as a factor of growth and retention. It is a fallacy that Freemasonry is expensive. It is simply not true because it does not have to be. We have created this conflict ourselves. This has a cascading effect at each level of the York Rite. The cost of membership seems to be different everywhere you go, and in many cases, the amount does not make sense. After the first year, Brothers can no longer afford $300 in annual dues for one organization and simply drift away without a word. As a factor of time, we create too many competing events for the organization; this becomes overtaxing for our members, and the conflict causes them to have to choose one thing over the other or participate in nothing at all. We can make the case that we have missed and lost a lot of good men because membership is not affordable. We can also make a case that men who can afford high membership costs are not necessarily good men for fraternity. A Brother who cannot afford to maintain membership in a Lodge cannot further advance in Freemasonry in the Chapter, Council, nor Commandery.

Though we look here through the lens of the Lodge, these pitfalls and challenges creep across the other York Rite organizations because of counterproductive practices and customs. Because of this, the York Rite, from the Lodge to the Chapter, from the Chapter to the Council, and from the Council through the Commandery, must operate as one organization. The importance of operating as one organization cannot be overstated. There must be clear leadership alignment and a collective effort. This must be reciprocal and be a matter of shared interests and responsibilities on the part of each leader of these organizations at every level of the fraternity.

A Lodge of Master Masons

The desire to establish the York Rite has to be a request of the Brothers of the Lodge and the objective of your Grand Chapter, Council, and Commandery. There needs to be an assessment of the Lodge's economic power, growth, retention rates, and geographical area to constitute the establishment of a Holy Royal Arch Chapter. It is common to operate on a rule of three with the rationale of having three Lodges supporting a Chapter. The build of one to three Chapters supports a Council, and the build of one to two Councils supports a Commandery. While three may provide ease of viability, the successful, consistent growth and retention of one can be enough. For this discussion, let's look at this through the build of one and three Lodges.

The Lodge's Growth. The Lodge is the basic building block of the Fraternity. It is the structure by which we operate as members. As a member, you are the Lodge and it is a living, functioning entity. You must take great care in your actions and decisions as far as what happens with your membership and the leadership of your Lodge. You are a leader and decision maker within your Lodge, and your actions, whether of good or bad consequence, directly impact the livelihood of your Lodge.

The viability and growth of the Lodge are critical to the whole of the York Rite. Think of your Lodge growth as a factor of economic power, men, and their talents and resources at the service of membership and community. With this in mind, the Lodge must display the best in conduct in both its community and membership-facing activities and leadership alignment. All bodies in Freemasonry have a sovereign geographic space in which they exist. Whether it be by country or province, jurisdiction or state, district or region, there is a sovereign operating space. Within every space, there should be concerns for growth and initiatives and objectives deliberately targeted at growth. Not necessarily solicitation, but established objectives for future growth and strategies to achieve such objectives. Every Lodge should have a like mindset about growth. How might a Lodge attract the interests of the right men? Not those of a particular wealth status, but the right men who are qualified and can bring their talents and resources for the betterment of the Lodge.

First, consider your external, community-facing aspect, your presence, and let us revisit our previous discussion on misrepresentation. Your masonic association will attract the interests of men throughout your personal and professional relationships and spaces. And how well you represent Freemasonry and your Lodge will make a difference. You must also have a positive operating presence in your geographic space. If it is your desire to expand across your geographic space, say your district or region, you have to go there (presence) in order to grow there. An adjustment here would be shirts with your masonic branding or logo. An alternate uniform away from the standard black and white suit. Think about the simplest activity—something like Brothers having lunch or dinner after meetings. Or meet up for Lodge community events.

Pick out new places in other towns or cities within your region or district and have a uniform presence wearing your branded shirt for lunch or dinner. Also look for new community events to participate in that are in other towns or cities within your geographical area. Through your community service events, work on establishing lasting relationships and an identity of dependability (what you become known for). When your community seeks out your Lodge, and that annual service event becomes an expectation from your community, your Lodge has arrived at establishing a positive presence and identity in your community. Again, you have to go there to grow there.

Second, consider your internal, Lodge, and fraternity-facing aspect, your Lodge environment, and let us revisit the administration and Lodge business. Your initial engagements with a potential candidate are a first and lasting impression. How well you investigate and interview a candidate should be taken as an equal evaluation of you and your Lodge. It is important to be organized, on time, and have a structured list of questions. Also consider having a Past Master lead this investigations committee. The impression you leave from your quality of work at ceremonies of initiation should also be seen as an evaluation of your Lodge. Here, the importance of a well-rehearsed and proficient degree team cannot be overstated. The work of the Lodge and the presence of the Lodge set the beginnings of what is to come for membership retention. Develop a sense of pride among Brothers in making the very best first impression in representing your Lodge and Freemasonry.

The Lodge's Membership Retention. A lot of things factor into membership retention. Think of the whole of a Brother's membership experience. What are we doing to make that experience a positive one, or should we improve upon it? If we work to retain them, then we don't have to reclaim them. The amount of work necessary to realize positive outcomes depends on the activity and environment of your Lodge. There are many practices and norms that have become counterproductive. There is the subject of a man's preparedness we assume away that might have an adverse impact within the Lodge. The result is often a loss in membership and even the loss of a Lodge. We must remember that we are dealing with human beings, and it is necessary to operate from the idea of promoting the well-being of our members and the operating health of the Lodge and internal environment. How might we maintain the interest of the good men we have attracted? What things might we change to improve that human experience, while supporting our growth and sustainment strategy?

First, consider activity post-altar, the Lodge's administration and business operations, and the need for engagement, involvement, and empowerment. Establish a training and education program and assign mentors. As with any other organization, it is an investment in the long game that pays off later with positive residual returns. This keeps the Brothers engaged, improves knowledge and skills, and hopefully, from a progressive standpoint, prepares the Lodge for sustainment in the future. As stated before, look at subject matter that covers things like the history of the fraternity, Grand Lodge and Lodge organization and governance structure, Lodge operations, masonic law, fraternal protocols, fraternal recognition, constitutions and bylaws, parliamentary procedures, and roles and responsibilities of members of the Lodge. Add on those committee and degree team assignments. This will help to keep Brothers interested and keep them engaged.

Make the extension of traveling and fraternal recognition a part of your member development. Visit other Lodges in your jurisdiction, region, and district, including those of other affiliations with fraternal recognition, and encourage open visitation as much as possible. The end state should be a well-informed, well-traveled Brother who can, through a process of maturation, make the best decisions for the Lodge and who can best apply himself in the best interest of the Lodge.

Second, consider the operating environment in your Lodge. Your Lodge environment needs to be one of inclusion, free and open discussion, sound business practices, and transparency. The presiding officer needs not mistake limited powers and responsibilities for absolute power and control over his Lodge. The top three or five officers of the Lodge need not mistake their positions to imply some form of executive power over the Lodge. There should be no exclusions or executive decisions in the Lodge. A presiding officer, top three or five exercising this type of control over the Lodge, will quickly lose the members of the Lodge. A lack of sound business practices and transparency will quickly erode members' confidence in the presiding officer's ability to lead the Lodge and therefore contribute to the loss of members.

The decision making of the Lodge rests solely on the members of the Lodge, and this is collectively every member of the Lodge. Brothers need to be set to work on behalf of the Lodge. It is not enough to just give a Brother something to do. The most important thing a Brother needs to understand is his decision-making power and responsibility to the Lodge. He must be present in order to ensure a voice is given to what happens with the Lodge and help the Lodge avoid common pitfalls and adverse practices. That means committees are at work, and training and development are happening.

The Lodge must have comprehensive bylaws, a solid trestle board with a strategic plan, and an approved budget. Without these, your Lodge has no direction. The Secretary and Treasurer must render timely, complete, and accurate reports. The committees provide information and recommendations to the Lodge members, and Lodge members make informed decisions about the choice of activities and expenditures of the Lodge. Brothers feel included and have open discussions, free of fear of influence, retribution, or retaliation. Give particular care to the Brothers who volunteer to use their talents for the interests of the Lodge or present a concern regarding Lodge operations. We have to always keep in mind that our membership is made up of professionals who are very intelligent and articulate. In our application process, we should consider a man's talents and how best the Lodge might use said talents. Do not set aside this Brother's request or ignore this Brother's concerns. You should operate your Lodge in a way that a Brother feels involved, valued, and appreciated, and in an atmosphere that captures the trust and confidence of any Brother present, even visitors.

Third, consider affordability of membership. A Brother interested in Freemasonry need not be told this is expensive. Because we make it expensive, we lose a lot of Brothers within the first one to two years because they cannot afford to continue to pay high rates for dues year after year. And they slip away from the Lodge without a word. We need to stop with the fallacy that dues need to be high because the Lodge needs money. Most of our Lodges don't even operate on an approved budget to help make sense of what the Lodge might need. We just come up with a number that sounds good, and whenever asked, the explanation sounds like a made-up number. Also, we need not engage in practices of recruitment of men who present a particular financial status that implies they can afford the high dues we set for the Lodge. We simply need to make Lodge dues affordable for any good, qualified man, regardless of an assumed financial status. Besides, a measure of financial wealth is not a qualification to become a Freemason.

Start by asking what the Lodge needs and prepare a budget. Typically, a Lodge will have operating costs (post office box, building, furniture) and service/charity costs (scholarships, grants, charity, service event costs) with income sources (dues and fundraisers). All membership-related administrative costs (certificates, dues cards, rituals, regalia, death gratuities) are covered by a member's initiation fee and Grand Lodge dues. The annual maintenance of such membership costs (death gratuities and dues cards) will continue to be covered by a member's payment of Grand Lodge dues. If it is a budget item for per-member tax, it balances out with the Grand Lodge.

If it is your first year, leverage everything you have available, including the talents of the Brothers in the Lodge. Though the membership costs will balance out, this should net a small amount of income from new members. For Lodge furniture, allow Brothers to donate things by dividing up purchases or making items. Establish awards to recognize Brothers' contributions to the Lodge, not the top three officers, but recognize other Brothers in the Lodge. For things like charity and scholarships, you should not go at these alone in the first year of the Lodge.

Leverage the scholarships through your Grand Lodge education programs and volunteers, and make connections through your local community service events. Cut these costs, and throw in a fundraiser for your Lodge. You want to make your dues make sense, and your Lodge Budget is the right place to start. Ask a question of how much money the Lodge needs on hand. Don't make up a number or make it excessive and appear overtaxing. Get rid of the adverse practices and give Brothers money back, to allow Brothers to keep more that they may retain some economic power to be able to support other matters of the Lodge as liberally as they can.

Let's look at an ideal budget for a Lodge. This budget is structured around common Lodge requirements, and the list of expenses and sources of income may differ from place to place. The minimal fee of $35 for Lodge dues is offered here for three reasons. As a matter of affordability, this small amount is enough for a Lodge to cover expenses, while making retention and economic power achievable. As a matter of value, the average membership experience in an organization is worth about $35 a year. As a matter of reality, somewhere a Grand level Chapter, Council, or Commandery's dues are as low as $35.

Year 1-2		Year 3 and Beyond	
Costs	-$3,825.00	Costs	-$5,575.00
Membership Reporting to GL Dues @$80 per/10	($800.00)	Membership Reporting to GL Dues @$80 per/30*	($2,400.00)
New Member Reporting to GL Dues @$85 per/10	($850.00)	New Member Reporting to GL Dues @$85 per/10	($850.00)
New Member Regalia @$65 per/10	($650.00)	New Member Regalia @$65 per/10	($650.00)
Post Office Box	($100.00)	Post Office Box	($100.00)
Sec./Tres. Supplies	($100.00)	Sec./Tres. Supplies	($50.00)
Building Maint.	($200.00)	Building Maint.	($200.00)
Furniture Maint.* Leverage Brother Donations	($600.00)	Furniture Maint.	($50.00)
Leverage GL Education/Scholarship Programs	$0.00	School Education Programs/Leverage GL Scholarships	($250.00)
Leverage Brother Donations for Charity	$0.00	Charity/Leverage Brothers Donations	($250.00)
Leverage Community-Volunteer Events	$0.00	Sevice Events/Awards	($250.00)
Grand Lodge Fees (Events, etc.)	($300.00)	Grand Lodge Fees (Events, etc.)	($300.00)
Annual Service Fees (Audit, etc.)	($225.00)	Annual Service Fees (Audit, etc.)	($225.00)
Income	$5,150.00	Income	$8,950.00
Membership Dues @$115 per/10*	$1,150.00	Membership Dues @$115 per/30*	$3,450.00
New Members @$250 per/10	$2,500.00	New Members @$250 per/10	$2,500.00
Fraternal Assistance	$500.00	Fraternal Assistance	$500.00
Fundraisers Total	$1,000.00	Fundraisers Total	$2,500.00
*Brothers can donate, make or buy furniture items; share costs		*Beyond Year 1 Growth and Retention critical to Lodge Income	
Dues Total ($115.00) is $80.00-Grand Lodge; **$35.00-Lodge		**Dues Total ($115.00) is $80.00-Grand Lodge; **$35.00-Lodge**	

If your Lodge is far beyond the first year and you are struggling to grow and retain your membership, look at the affordability of your dues from year to year. If your Lodge is down to only five to eight Brothers consistently attending meetings and events, do not assume this away as the faithful few. This is a sign that change is needed. It is a bad practice to punish the Brothers who remain by increasing dues just because of the Lodge's failure to grow and retain membership. We are talking affordability, but also look at the external community-facing and internal business operations for the Lodge. There may be a need to cut your operating costs and retool at square one with the focus of a Lodge in year one. Cut back on some things and tailor all activities to what makes sense for the number of Brothers you have.

Nothing requires us to award $1,000 scholarships to college students or expend a certain amount of money on charity. Instead, consider an alternative that we can achieve a greater and lasting impact with less by helping five hundred underrepresented, underprivileged, or at-risk students in our elementary, middle, and high schools. Another way is to do joint community service events with other organizations to maintain a presence, while not having to do the work of planning, sponsoring, or executing events. There is nothing wrong with coming up with a fundraiser or two.

In an effort to retain the Brothers you have, consider resetting your budget, cutting costs, and reducing dues to give money back if you can, prioritizing things like awards to ensure you can still recognize Brothers' work in the Lodge. The idea is that you retain those you have and put a bit of economic power back into their pockets. Again, you are giving money back and making it affordable for Brothers to still be in the room. It is better to have fifty members who can afford $35 in Lodge dues a year than it is to have only seven members who can afford $170 in Lodge dues a year. Once a Brother is in the room, you can get him to support anything after that. A room of fifty Brothers can each afford to give $5 ($250) at any time for any cause, while the setting of only seven Brothers may feel overtaxed and cannot afford to do any more for the Lodge, or maybe, if able to afford $5, they will never carry the same economic power of fifty at the drop of a hat.

Here is an example of how a Lodge might look that is struggling due to affordability as compared to the look of a Lodge with affordability and greater economic power, with a larger work/participating force and resources. This next table suggests that affordable dues at $35 for twenty Brothers ($700 + $2,280 = $2,980) are greater than the economic power of nine Brothers at $170 ($1,530) in a struggling Lodge. This idea of affordability also suggests that if both Lodges start with twenty members, the Lodge whose dues are $170 will continue to see a decline and inconsistent progress in its economic power. We will discuss economic power in greater detail later.

Lodge A

$170	$170		$170
$170			
$170		$170	
$170			
$170			$170

E-Power: 7 (available to work)
E-Power: 9 (pay dues)/$1,530
E-Plus: None

OR

Lodge B

$35	$35	$35	$35
$35	$35	$35	$35
$35	$35	$35	$35
$35	$35	$35	$35
$35	$35	$35	$35

E-Power: 19 (available to work)
E-Power: 20 (pay dues)/$700
E-Plus: 19 x $10 X (12 causes)/$2,280

If you desire growth and sustainability for the York Rite, then membership affordability should be a key component of your membership strategy. A point to your strategy here is to leave more money in a Brother's pocket, so that he might afford to give to the Lodge liberally wherever the Lodge might need support for other causes. Another point is you want Brothers to continue membership beyond the first two years of membership. It is also important to think of the other fraternal organizations that depend on the Lodge's members for their existence. The consideration for reducing dues and making them affordable has no bearing on your candidate application process. Affording a higher threshold for dues does not equate to the quality of the men being admitted to your organization. You are also making it affordable for a Brother to continue his knowledge and development in Freemasonry if seeking membership to a Chapter, Council, and Commandery. And you are building the Lodge with the Commandery in mind.

The Economic Power of the Lodge. To continue in the vein of growth and retention and our obsession with money, think of the idea of growing the economic power of your Lodge. Think of your Lodge population as a division of labor and resources which serves your community to bring about positive social change in the name of Freemasonry. Also consider the matter of attrition due to death, age and mobility, transfers, affordability, lack of interest, dissatisfaction, and lack of participation as these relate to the growth and sustainment of your Lodge's economic power for the good of the York Rite. To measure economic power, take the number of Brothers present to work in the Lodge (work/labor/participation) and then the number of dues paid to the Lodge by Brothers both present and not present in the Lodge (financial resources).

Economic power increases with a Brother's affordability to pay dues and also give liberally to any cause of the Lodge while participating in most activities of the Lodge. Economic power decreases when a Brother can afford to pay dues but cannot afford to give any more to the Lodge, while also not participating in many activities. Here is an illustration of potential increase and then degradation in economic power due to affordability, growth, and retention:

Lodge A Year 1

$170	$170	$170	$170
$170	$170	$170	$170
$170	$170	$170	$170
$170	$170	$170	$170
$170	$170	$170	$170

E-Power: 20 (available to work)
E-Power: 20 (pay dues)/$3,400

Lodge A Year 2

$170	$170	$170		$170
$170	$170	$170		$170
$170	$170			$170
$170	$170			$170
$170	$170			$170

E-Power: 13 (available to work)
E-Power: 17 (pay dues)/$2,890

Lodge A Year 3

$170	$170			$170
$170				$170
$170			$170	$170
$170				$170
$170	$170			$170

E-Power: 8 (available to work)
E-Power: 13 (pay dues)/$2,210

We can see how the economic power of the Lodge might be limited to those Brothers who can afford to pay dues. These same Brothers may not be able to afford to do anything more for the Lodge. From year to year, your Lodge will endure some kind of change. In this illustration a Lodge might begin with twenty members in Year 1 and, for reasons previously stated, may bring in five new members through the inner door while losing twelve members through the other door. The Lodge's economic power is based on the number of Brothers actively participating in the business of the Lodge and the financial resources reflective of dues paid. There will be instances where a Brother will pay dues but not participate in much of the Lodge's business due to personal choice or conflict.

In Year 2 you have eight who leave and four who no longer participate but still pay their dues ($170). Likewise, in Year 3, the Lodge can regain six new members while losing five who leave and five who no longer participate but still pay their dues. Here, your Lodge goes through the ebb and flow of twenty to thirteen members in a three-year span and an overall negative growth trend. Usually, a progression of lack of participation but paying dues is followed by leaving without saying a word and then nonpayment of dues. The issue of affordability, lack of interest, dissatisfaction, and lack of participation can be addressed by the Lodge, and the Lodge members should inquire of a Brother regarding his decision to leave the Lodge.

We can also see this illustrated in a different way if one or more Lodges are struggling with growth and retention, and issues with community-facing and membership experience. We can make a case that the overall population of the Lodges may still provide some sense of viability to establish a Royal Arch Chapter, but affordability and other common issues will likely continue to plague the Lodges and spread to the Chapter as well. We are likely to repeat the same customary practice of making the Chapter dues as high as those of the Lodge.

Lodge A

$170	$170	$170	$170
$170	$170	$170	$170
$170	$170	$170	$170
$170	$170		
$170	$170		

E-Power: 13(available to work)
E-Power: 16(pay dues)/$2,720

Lodge B

$170	$170	$170		$170
$170	$170	$170		$170
$170	$170			$170
$170	$170			$170
$170	$170			$170

E-Power: 13(available to work)
E-Power: 17(pay dues)/$2,890

Lodge C

$170	$170		$170
$170			$170
$170		$170	$170
$170			$170
$170	$170		$170

E-Power: 8(available to work)
E-Power: 13(pay dues)/$2,210

....

Chapter A Year 1

$100	$100	$100
$100	$100	$100
$100	$100	$100
$100	$100	$100

E-Power: 12 (available to work)
E-Power: 12 (pay dues)/$1,200

Chapter A Year 2

$100	$100	$100
$100	$100	$100
$100		$100
$100	$100	$100

E-Power: 10 (available to work)
E-Power: 11 (pay dues)/$1,100

Chapter A Year 3

$100	$100	$100	$100
$100	$100	$100	$100
$100	$100		$100
$100	$100		$100

E-Power:11 (available to work)
E-Power: 14 (pay dues)/$1,400

Like the Lodge, year to year, your Chapter will endure some kind of attrition. In this illustration, your Chapter might begin with fifteen members in Year 1. Due to the same pitfalls and challenges previously stated, you may not bring in any new members through Year 2, and then lose two Companions back to the Lodge who can either no longer participate because of time conflicts, but still pay both their dues ($170 + $100 = $270), or who cannot afford to pay dues for both organizations. Then, in Year 3, the Chapter can bring in four new members while losing five back to the Lodge who can no longer participate but still pay their dues or can no longer afford to pay dues at all. Here is how a Chapter might struggle while being sustained by a struggling Lodge or struggling Lodges. In the same vein, issues of affordability, lack of interest, dissatisfaction, and lack of participation can be addressed at the Lodge and Chapter levels, but this is where operating pitfalls, leadership alignment, and affordability strategies need to be considered.

We can also see this illustrated in a different way if a Lodge is addressing growth and retention issues, making dues affordable, and avoiding common pitfalls and challenges and fostering a positive community-facing and membership experience. Consider where affordability is a retention strategy, but the Lodge still faces common issues with attrition due to death, age and mobility, transfers, lack of interest, dissatisfaction, and lack of participation. Here you may have Brothers who choose to still pay their dues to the Lodge while participating more in, say, the Royal Arch Chapter. And they continue to support the Lodge by paying dues because it is affordable to do so.

Lodge A Year 1

$35	$35	$35	$35
$35	$35	$35	$35
$35	$35	$35	$35
$35	$35	$35	$35
$35	$35	$35	$35

E-Power: 20 (work)/$700(20-dues)
E-Plus: 20 (work)/$2,400(contribute)

Lodge A Year 2

$35	$35			$35
$35	$35	$35	$35	$35
$35	$35	$35	$35	$35
$35	$35	$35	$35	$35
$35	$35	$35	$35	$35

E-Power: 22 (work)/$770 (23-dues)
E-Plus: 22 (work)/$2,640(contribute)

Lodge A Year 3

$35	$35	$35	$35	$35	$35	$35
$35	$35	$35	$35	$35	$35	$35
$35	$35	$35	$35	$35	$35	$35
$35	$35	$35	$35	$35	$35	$35
	$35	$35	$35	$35	$35	$35

E-Power: 31 (work)/$1,155 (33-dues)
E-Plus: 31 (work)/$3,720 (contribute)

OR

Lodge A

$35	$35	$35	$35	$35
$35	$35	$35	$35	$35
$35	$35	$35	$35	$35
$35	$35	$35	$35	$35
$35	$35	$35	$35	$35
		$35	$35	$35
$35	$35	$35	$35	$35

E-Power: 31 (work)/$1,155(33-dues)
E-Plus: 31 (work)/$3,720(contribute)

Lodge B

$35	$35	$35	$35	$35	$35
$35	$35	$35	$35	$35	$35
$35	$35	$35	$35	$35	$35
$35	$35	$35	$35	$35	$35
$35	$35	$35	$35	$35	$35
$35		$35	$35	$35	$35
$35	$35	$35	$35	$35	$35

E-Power: 38 (work)/$1,435(41-dues)
E-Plus: 38 (work)/$4,560(contribute)

Lodge C

$35	$35	$35	$35	$35	$35
$35	$35	$35	$35	$35	$35
$35	$35	$35	$35	$35	$35
$35	$35	$35	$35	$35	$35
$35	$35	$35	$35	$35	$35
$35	$35	$35	$35	$35	$35
$35	$35	$35			

E-Power: 37 (work)/$1,365(39-dues)
E-Plus: 37 (work)/$4,440(contribute)

And to this illustration, the fallacy that the organization needs money can be satisfied by doing the very opposite of what has been detrimental to our growth and retention rates. Reduce Lodge dues and give Brothers money back and leave more money in a Brother's pocket, making membership affordable and sustainable for not just two years but twenty years. The Lodge should also realize an increase in economic power through the increased number of Brothers who can afford to be in the Lodge room from year to year.

The plus in economic power can be expressed as the number of Brothers present to work who can give $5–$10 to any cause (one cause per month) of the Lodge, as their financial circumstance allows. By doing this you will have Brothers who can afford to give far more of what is asked, where some Brothers might only be able to afford to give $5–$10, at times, you have Brothers who will give $25–$100 or more at any given time for the Lodge. And you should not care about who is giving $5 as compared to who is giving $50 or how many times. Your main priority is building and sustaining the economic power in the room to carry out the business of the Lodge and Freemasonry. This is far more economically powerful than trying to recover the economic loss of the Brothers who, with dues at $170, deemed too high, can no longer continue to pay them.

The gist here is to allow members to donate money for things like furniture and equipment as liberally as their individual economic situations might allow. We often talk about needing money without ever even having a budget. As an alternative, and with economic power, allow a Brother to voluntarily purchase an item, make an item, or donate money for an item. By allowing a Brother to give as his economic situation allows, you are giving a Brother full latitude to support the Lodge without forcing him to pay an arbitrary amount that he may not be able to afford. A Brother may not be able to purchase and donate an altar cloth, but he may be able to buy a gavel, and that may be the limits of his finances at that time. It provides for a higher sustained volume of members in the organization and creates greater sustained economic power of the organization.

Again, if a Brother can continue to afford to be in the room, you can get him to serve and support any other cause in the Lodge. This also provides greater viability for the establishment of a Royal Arch Chapter. The ability to sustain one or two Chapters greatly improves with consistent positive growth of one or more Lodges. Another thing to bear in mind is that this approach also prevents a Brother from growing resentful when he feels forced to do something he might not be able to afford. It may cause shame and conflict with his family and induce a Brother to drift away from the Lodge.

We can also see this illustrated in a different way if a Lodge and Chapter are both aligned and are addressing growth and retention issues or avoiding common pitfalls and challenges and fostering a positive community-facing and membership experience. Only the Lodge has a community-facing presence in the true meaning of the word, as it draws its membership from that community. The Chapter's direct community face, in a sense, is the Lodge. Consider where affordability is a retention strategy, but the Lodge and Chapter still face common issues with attrition due to death, age and mobility, transfers, lack of interest, dissatisfaction, and lack of participation. Here, as with the Lodge, you may have Brothers who choose to still pay their dues to the Chapter while participating more in Lodge activities. And they continue to pay dues to support both organizations because it is affordable. Though the organizations may experience a slight degradation in labor, a continued adjustment on behalf of the Lodge to improve the quality of community-facing and membership activities, while making membership affordable, will ensure the viability and sustainment of the York Rite. If we work to retain them, then we don't have to reclaim them.

Lodge A

$35	$35	$35	$35	$35
$35	$35	$35	$35	$35
$35	$35	$35	$35	$35
$35	$35	$35	$35	$35
$35	$35	$35	$35	$35
		$35	$35	$35
$35	$35	$35	$35	$35

E-Power: 31 (work)/$1,188(33-dues)
E-Plus: 31 (work)/$3,480(contribute)

Lodge B

$35	$35	$35	$35	$35	$35
$35	$35	$35	$35	$35	$35
$35	$35	$35	$35	$35	$35
$35	$35	$35	$35	$35	$35
$35	$35	$35	$35	$35	$35
$35		$35	$35	$35	$35
$35	$35	$35	$35	$35	$35

E-Power: 38 (work)/$1,404(41-dues)
E-Plus: 37 (work)/$4,440(contribute)

Lodge C

$35	$35	$35	$35	$35	$35
$35	$35	$35	$35	$35	$35
$35	$35	$35	$35	$35	$35
$35	$35	$35	$35	$35	$35
$35	$35	$35	$35	$35	$35
$35	$35	$35	$35	$35	$35

E-Power: 34 (work)/$1,296(36-dues)
E-Power: 34 (work)/$4,080(contribute)

Chapter A Year 1

$35	$35	$35	$35
$35	$35	$35	$35
$35	$35	$35	$35
$35	$35	$35	$35
$35	$35	$35	$35

Chapter A Year 2

$35	$35	$35	$35	$35	$35	$35
$35	$35	$35	$35	$35	$35	$35
$35	$35	$35	$35	$35	$35	$35
$35	$35	$35	$35	$35	$35	$35
$35	$35	$35	$35	$35	$35	$35

Chapter A Year 3

$35	$35	$35	$35	$35	$35	$35	$35
$35	$35	$35	$35	$35	$35	$35	$35
$35	$35	$35	$35	$35	$35	$35	$35
$35	$35	$35	$35	$35	$35	$35	$35
$35	$35	$35	$35	$35	$35	$35	$35
$35	$35	$35	$35	$35	$35	$35	$35

The Health of the Lodge. As your Lodge goes through population changes, evaluate the health of your Lodge or Lodges. For the health of your Lodge, consider the number of members in and the number of members out as a matter of growth/turnover and retention in a given year. Using a growth rate and a retention rate is a good way to measure the health of your organization. This can be useful at any level of the organization, for any one or multiple organizations in a geographical area.

To measure **Growth Rate**, subtract the number of members at the beginning of the year from the number of members at the end of the year, then divide that number by the number of members at the end of the year.

Finally, multiply that number by one hundred. If the difference between the ending and beginning numbers is negative, then your growth will be negative. It is likely this is already an annual reporting mechanism for the Lodge. As an example, if at the beginning of 2018, your Lodge membership was forty-six members (assuming your loss was zero members), and your end-of-year membership was fifty-two, your growth rate is expressed as:

Growth = 52 (end-of-year number) – 46 (begin of year number) = 6 (difference),
then 6/52 (end-of-year number = 0.115 (percentage of difference-decimal)
then 0.115 x 100 = 11.5 or 12 percent in positive growth.
OR a loss of six members,
Growth = 46 (end-of-year number) – 52 (begin of year number) = -6 (difference),
then -6/52 (end-of-year number = 0.115 (percentage of difference-decimal)
then -0.115 x 100 = -11.5 or -12 percent in negative growth.

To measure **Retention Rate**, take the number of members lost during the year from the number of members at the beginning of the year, say forty-six. Do not include the number of net new members for that year; those would be included for growth. As an example, for retention, if at the beginning of 2018, your Lodge membership was forty-six members and you lost two members through some manner of attrition due to death, age and mobility, transfers, affordability, lack of interest, dissatisfaction, and lack of participation, your retention rate is expressed as:

Retention = 46 (beginning number) – 2 (number of loss) = 44 (ending number),
then (44/46) x 100 = 0.956 or 96 percent retention rate, which is significantly high.

These are considerations for assessing the health of your Lodge. A consistent positive growth rate for the Lodge that is equal to or greater than 25 percent allows the Lodge the ability to support the growth of the

York Rite with little impact from the pitfalls of things like misrepresentation and perversion, and community-facing activities. This shows the Lodge's capacity to grow the economic power to be able to better serve its community without strain on the membership. A consistent retention rate equal to or greater than 85 percent allows the Lodge the ability to support the growth of the York Rite with little impact from community and membership-facing activities and affordability. This shows the Lodge's capacity to provide a satisfying membership experience and retain its economic power. A growth rate of less than 25 percent would make sustainment tough in the long run. A Lodge retention rate of less than 75 percent runs counters to the 25 percent growth rate needed to support and sustain growth across the York Rite.

A Chapter of Holy Royal Arch Masons

THE CHAPTER WILL BE subject to the same pitfalls and challenges as the Lodge in the way in which it operates as an organization in both its community and membership-facing activities. The Chapter still needs to be concerned with misrepresentation and perversion, fraternal politics, membership interests and satisfaction, training and development, leadership development and alignment, and affordability. Once established, there needs to be a continuous assessment of the Chapter's economic power, growth and retention rates, and geographical area to constitute the establishment of a Council. Again, a Council can be deemed viable through the support of one or more Chapters.

The Chapter's Growth. The viability and growth of the Chapter hinge on the population of the Lodge or Lodges in its geographical footprint. Like the Lodge, the Chapter must display the best in conduct in both its community and membership-facing activities and leadership alignment. The Chapter will also have its jurisdiction designated by district, region, or province, as a sovereign space, but the Chapter must not operate in a way that is exclusive of the Lodges of its jurisdiction operating in the same space. With the addition of the Chapter, leadership alignment is most important. There should be a desire to establish a Chapter or growth and recruitment initiatives and objectives particular to the Chapter. The Lodge will provide a population pool of qualified Brothers to establish, grow, and sustain the Chapter.

The Chapter membership should reflect a volume of equal to or greater than 25 percent of the Lodge population or the overall population of all Lodges. There may be a minimum of nine members required to constitute a Chapter, but this number may be set to twelve or fifteen. It should be expected that it may take one Lodge some time to grow the membership needed to support the idea of having a Chapter, while it may not take as long if a Chapter is to be supported by three Lodges. Here is an example and illustration of forming a Chapter through one or three Lodges:

Lodge A Year 1 (20)

LG	LG	LG	CH
LG	LG	LG	CH
LG	LG	LG	CH
LG	LG	LG	CH
LG	LG	LG	CH

25 percent (5) is not enough to warrant a Chapter.

Lodge A Year 2 (25)

LG	LG	LG	LG	CH
LG	LG	LG	LG	CH
LG	LG	LG	LG	CH
LG	LG	LG	CH	CH
LG	LG	LG	CH	CH

25 percent (6) with a little growth is not enough to warrant a Chapter.

Lodge A Year 3 (40)

LG	LG	LG	LG	LG	LG	CH	CH
LG	LG	LG	LG	LG	LG	CH	CH
LG	LG	LG	LG	LG	LG	CH	CH
LG	LG	LG	LG	LG	LG	CH	CH
LG	LG	LG	LG	LG	LG	CH	CH

25 percent (10) near minimum is enough to warrant a Chapter.

OR

Lodge A (36)

LG	LG	LG	LG	LG	LG
LG	LG	LG	LG	LG	LG
LG	LG	LG	LG	LG	LG
LG	LG	CH	CH	CH	CH
LG	LG	CH	CH	CH	CH
LG	LG	LG	LG	LG	LG

Lodge B (42)

LG	LG	CH	CH	CH	LG	LG
LG	LG	CH	CH	CH	LG	LG
LG	LG	CH	CH	CH	LG	LG
LG	LG	CH	LG	LG	LG	LG
LG	LG	LG	LG	LG	LG	LG
LG	LG	LG	LG	LG	LG	LG

Lodge C (30)

LG	LG	LG	LG	LG	LG
LG	LG	LG	LG	LG	LG
LG	LG	LG	CH	CH	CH
LG	LG	LG	CH	CH	CH
LG	LG	LG	CH	CH	CH

Chapter A (27)

CH	CH	CH	CH	CH
CH	CH	CH	CH	CH
CH	CH	CH	CH	CH
CH	CH	CH	CH	CH
CH	CH	CH	CH	CH
CH	CH			

Establish a Chapter with 25 percent (27) of your overall Lodge population.

Here, a single Lodge may not have the growth needed to constitute a Chapter. Even where the slightest of growth might provide what appears to be sufficient numbers, use the minimum number needed to constitute the organization first, then keep the measure of 25 percent as a buffer. Also consider using a reasonable factor of three (three times the minimum needed) to add a greater buffer to pursue a higher-than-needed membership volume. Understanding the number required to constitute the Chapter is most important. It is best to wait until the population of the Lodge or Lodges is ready and has the capacity to support a Chapter. The addition of a buffer ensures the Chapter can sustain itself through the first three years or so until it can start to realize consistent positive growth. In using a rule of three, whereby three Lodges form a pipeline to one Chapter, then establishment and growth might not be as challenging as that encountered by one Lodge, one pipeline. The idea of three Lodges and three pipelines to one Chapter does provide some complexity for alignment.

Just as with the Lodge, consider your internal Chapter and fraternity-facing aspect, your Chapter administration and business environment. Your initial engagements with a potential Companion are a first and lasting impression. It is still equally of importance to have a well-rehearsed and proficient degree team. Like the Lodge, the work of the Chapter and the presence of the Chapter sets the beginnings of what is to come for membership retention. Develop a sense of cooperation and alignment with the Lodge. The presiding officers and leadership should be in constant communication and working to ensure the pipeline from the Lodge, so to speak, is clear of conflict and competing interests.

The Chapter's Membership Retention. A Companion's membership experience in the Chapter is equally important as a Brother's experience in the Lodge. The amount of work necessary to realize positive outcomes now depends on the activities and environment of both the Chapter and the Lodge. As an immediate consideration to retention, just like the Lodge, the Chapter should be concerned with a Companion's preparedness to lead the Chapter, because this will have an adverse impact within the Chapter. The result of an adverse impact is the same, a loss in membership and even the loss of a Chapter. Here, it is necessary to promote the well-being of your members and the operating health of the Chapter and internal environment. Your Chapter environment needs to be one of inclusion, free and open discussion, sound business practices, and transparency. It is worth repeating that the decision making of the Chapter rests solely on the members of the Chapter, and this is collectively every member of the Chapter. How might you maintain the interest of the good Brothers and not compete with the Lodge?

The Chapter's administration and business operations need engagement, involvement, and empowerment. Like the Lodge, establish a training and education program specific to the Chapter. The transition from the Lodge into the Chapter can be somewhat challenging, so this is an area in which a mentor will add great value. This keeps the Brothers engaged and improves upon existing knowledge and skills. In addition to subject matters being taught in the Lodge, the Chapter covers things specific to the Chapter, like constitutions and bylaws, roles and responsibilities of members, and committee and degree team assignments. This will further help to keep interest and keep Brothers engaged.

As with the Lodge, make the extension of traveling and fraternal recognition a part of your member development. Visit other Chapters in your jurisdiction, region, and district, including those of other affiliations with fraternal recognition, and open visitation as much as possible. This will prove to be of greater value to a newly constituted Chapter. The end state should still be a well-informed, well-traveled Brother who can, through a process of maturation, make the best decisions for the Chapter and best apply himself in the best interest of the Chapter.

The Importance of Leadership Alignment. With the idea of the Chapter added, it is important to discuss leadership alignment. Leadership alignment is the alignment of all operating matters associated with the Lodge and the Chapter to which the York Rite might operate as one organization. Leadership alignment requires collective teamwork, cohesion, collaboration, cooperation, assistance, and a sense of shared interest and responsibility to ensure the harmony and sustainment of the York Rite. The two driving factors for alignment will always be time and money. They will always be time and money. There are some things that are central to the operation of all organizations and though complicated, but leaders have to be willing to cooperate, open their minds, and be willing to do something different, especially in cases where organizations are visibly struggling.

Lodge A		
LG	LG	LG
LG	LG	LG
LG	LG	LG

Lodge B		
LG	LG	LG
LG	LG	LG
LG	LG	LG

Lodge C		
LG	LG	LG
LG	LG	LG
LG	LG	LG

Chapter A		
CH	CH	CH
CH	CH	CH
CH	CH	CH
CH	CH	CH

OR

just through,

Lodge A

LG	LG	LG	LG
LG	LG	LG	LG
LG	LG	LG	LG
LG	LG	LG	LG

Meetings. Each organization will conduct its business meetings. We know it is likely each organization will have twelve meetings a year (one per month), if not twenty-four meetings (two per month with degree work). When you have Brothers who are members of both the Lodge and Chapter, this now becomes twenty-four or thirty-six or forty-eight meeting events in a year in order to participate in meetings of both organizations. To align on time from one Lodge to one Chapter will not be as complicated as aligning with Chapter members across three Lodges. This also amplifies conflicts with time and other personal obligations. It would be a little less conflicted if each had only twelve business meetings, but this is likely not the case. The Lodge comes first, so it is first to shape the conditions for meetings in its trestle board.

How might you reduce your Lodge's regular business meetings? This may be a practice in some Lodges already. Consolidate business and degree work into one meeting, giving the Lodge twelve meetings. Then create a degree schedule by quarter, where the first month of the quarter is for the first degree and so on. If a petition comes in the middle of the quarter, the Lodge should action it for the next cycle if time permits, but avoid shuffling the Lodge to react to a petition. You may also consider a summer break, whereas in the summer months, there is no degree work. What is offered up here for the Lodge is to make things in the Lodge predictable, manage member expectations, and give Brothers and their families time back.

The Lodge(s) and the Chapter both have to take all of these things into consideration for their respective organizations. The Chapter members should keep in mind the Lodge meeting date. When there is only one Lodge aligned with a Chapter, this is easy to manage, and with multiple Lodges, not so much. In all cases, the Chapter will intentionally schedule its regular meetings on a day different from that of the Lodges. Everybody cannot schedule their meetings on Saturdays. The idea is for working Brothers to have weekends and summer breaks to spend with family. In a situation where the Chapter and the Lodge schedule meetings on the same Saturday, this can simply be a Meeting Saturday where only one day and one Saturday are impacted. It requires that one meeting is scheduled after the other to avoid conflict and realize the value of the arrangement. The Chapter may not have as many iterations for Royal Arch degree work, as this could span a four-month extended quarter, two months, or one day. So, degree work one or two times a year is ideal for a Chapter.

Community Service Events. The Lodge will likely have several events already on its trestle board or calendar. Because it is common to have a Lodge and Chapter operating in the same space, there may be the same Brothers in the same organizations and this matter of division of labor needs to be leveraged and exploited to the maximum extent practical. The Brothers of the Lodge participating in the local food bank event are now also Companions of the Chapter. So, the Chapter does not have to create a separate event. The annual food bank event is now narrated as, "Eight Brothers of Lodges A and B, and eight Companions from Chapter A supported the Kansas City Food Bank on September 16, 2018," with a photo and Lodge and Chapter branding. Each Lodge and the Chapter report this participation in their monthly, quarterly, or annual reports.

If the masons in your geographical area have a positive presence and are known and expected to participate in certain events, continue to focus on those events and do not add any more events. Also consider co-sponsoring and doing joint events with what you already have. In some cases where fundraising is involved, remember the same men belong to each organization, so there is no advantage to thinking selfishly here. It would be expected that the Chapter may have one dedicated fundraiser. Again, you do not have to create separate events just for the Chapter to have something to do. Just work together. A Lodge and or Chapter that tries to continue to operate separately will struggle alone. This will surely create conflict and competing interests for Brothers'/Companions' time and other obligations.

Affordability. We discussed the idea of making dues affordable, and this does not necessarily require a lot for alignment. Each organization may approach money and affordability differently. Though this may solely be at the discretion of the members, it does require great consideration for the York Rite as one organization. When it comes to cutting costs associated with membership and activities of the organization, it is important to leverage existing resources and cut any net new programs or activities that will cause the Chapter or Lodge to incur additional costs.

Geographic Space. The geographic operating space also plays a role in leadership alignment as something that can help or add an element of complication. The York Rite is commonly structured under district integrity. That is, District 9's York Rite consists of thirteen Lodges, seven Chapters, four Councils, and four Commanderys of all the same members. Where you have a Lodge, Chapter, Council, and Commandery under the same geographic area and authority of a district, you can achieve ease of alignment regardless of how many separate organizations you have, especially if your district has a single dedicated meeting space for all masonic organizations. When a Chapter is formed by members of multiple districts, this becomes a factor of complication.

When the Council or Commandery is formed by members of multiple districts, it further complicates alignment and can make it impossible to achieve. Given that the leaders of these districts might have differing leadership perspectives for their Lodges or the Chapter, this could interfere with the growth and sustainability of the York Rite. Where the leadership construct of the Chapter, Council, and Commandery is totally separate from the district (Lodges), this too is an added problem for alignment. If the Lodges are operating under districts and the Chapters are operating under regions or provinces, the operating structure in itself runs counter to achieving alignment. It would be evident that leaders at the highest levels of the organizations are not aligned across the York Rite. Again, this would make alignment nearly unachievable for members of the Lodges, Chapters, Councils, and Commanderys as they would all see themselves as different and exclusive of the other because of how the York Rite is misaligned geographically with an intertwined authority structure. We usually design these top-down without much consideration for effects and conflicts at the ground level.

The Economic Power of the Chapter. There needs to be equal consideration given to the economic power of the Chapter. Again, think of your Chapter's population as a division of labor and resources, which serves your community to bring about positive social change in the name of Freemasonry. Also consider the matter of attrition due to death, age and mobility, transfers, affordability, lack of interest, dissatisfaction, and lack of participation as these relate to the growth and sustainment of your Chapter's economic power for the good of the York Rite. Economic power increases with a Brother's affordability to give liberally to any cause of the Chapter while participating in most activities of the Chapter. Economic power decreases when a Brother cannot afford to give any more to the Chapter while not participating in many activities of the Chapter. Here is an illustration of potential in economic power:

Lodge A

$170	$170	$170	$170
$170	$170	$170	$170
$170	$170	$170	$170
$170	$170		
$170	$170		

E-Power: 13 (available to work)
E-Power: 16 (pay dues)/$2,720

Lodge B

$170	$170	$170		$170
$170	$170	$170		$170
$170	$170			$170
$170	$170			$170
$170	$170			$170

E-Power: 13 (available to work)
E-Power: 17 (pay dues)/$2,890

Lodge C

$170	$170		$170
$170			$170
$170		$170	$170
$170			$170
$170	$170		$170

E-Power: 8 (available to work)
E-Power: 13 (pay dues)/$2,210

Chapter A Year 1

$100	$100	$100
$100	$100	$100
$100	$100	$100
$100	$100	$100

E-Power: 12 (available to work)
E-Power: 12 (pay dues)/$1,200

Chapter A Year 2

$100	$100	$100
$100	$100	$100
$100		$100
$100	$100	$100

E-Power: 10 (available to work)
E-Power: 11 (pay dues)/$1,100

Chapter A Year 3

$100	$100	$100	$100
$100	$100	$100	$100
$100	$100		$100
$100	$100		$100

E-Power: 11 (available to work)
E-Power: 14 (pay dues)/$1,400

We can see how the economic power of the Chapter might also be limited to those Companions who can afford to pay dues. Like before, these same Companions may not be able to afford to do anything more for the Chapter. The Chapter, too, from year to year, endures some kind of change. In this illustration, a Chapter might begin with fifteen members in Year 1 and may not bring in any members in Year 1. In Year 2 you have two who leave to participate only in the Lodge, but one Companion still pays his dues ($170 + 100 = $270). Later, in Year 3, the Chapter brings in five new members while losing four Companions who only want to participate in the Lodge, but two still pay their dues, while one is being lost by both the Chapter and the Lodge. The Chapter will continue to face the same challenges. A progression of lack of participation, but paying dues, is followed by leaving, and then nonpayment of dues. These issues can be addressed at the Chapter.

We can also see this illustrated in a different way if one or more Chapters or Lodges are challenged with growth and retention, and issues with community-facing and membership experience. As presented before, the overall population of the Chapters may provide some sense of viability to establish a Royal Select Council, but affordability and other common issues will likely continue to plague the Lodges and Chapters and spread to the Councils, and in the same vein, we are likely to repeat the same customary practice of making the Council dues as high as those of the Chapter and the Lodge.

Lodge A

$170	$170	$170	$170
$170	$170	$170	$170
$170	$170	$170	$170
$170	$170		
$170	$170		

E-Power: 13 (available to work)
E-Power: 16 (pay dues)/$2,720
E-Plus: None

Lodge B

$170	$170	$170		$170
$170	$170	$170		$170
$170	$170			$170
$170	$170			$170
$170	$170			$170

E-Power: 13 (available to work)
E-Power: 17 (pay dues)/$2,890

Lodge C

$170	$170		$170
$170			$170
$170		$170	$170
$170			$170
$170	$170		$170

E-Power: 8 (available to work)
E-Power: 13 (pay dues)/$2,210

Chapter A

$100	$100	$100
$100	$100	
$100		
$100	$100	$100

E-Power: 9 (available to work)
E-Power: 9 (pay dues)/$900
E-Plus: None

Chapter B

$100		$100
	$100	
	$100	$100
$100		$100
$100	$100	

E-Power: 8 (available to work)
E-Power: 9 (pay dues)/$900

Chapter C

	$100	$100	$100
	$100	$100	$100
$100	$100	$100	$100
$100			$100
			$100

E-Power: 10 (available to work)
E-Power: 13 (pay dues)/$1,300

We can view this in another way if the Lodge and Chapter are addressing growth and retention issues or avoiding common pitfalls and challenges and fostering a positive community-facing and membership experience. Consider where affordability is a retention strategy, but the Lodge and Chapter still face common issues with attrition due to death, age and mobility, transfers, lack of interest, dissatisfaction, and lack of participation. It is not uncommon for Brothers to decide on some degree of participation due to conflicts created across each of the organizations. This is, again, why alignment is important. You may have Brothers and Companions who choose to still pay their dues to the Lodge and Chapter while participating more in, say, the Council. And they continue to support the Lodge, Chapter, and Council by paying dues because it is affordable to do so.

Chapter A Year 1

$35	$35	$35
$35	$35	$35
$35	$35	$35
$35	$35	$35
$35	$35	$35

E-Power: 15 (work)/$525(15-dues)
E-Plus: 15 (work)/$1,800(contribute)

Chapter A Year 2

$35	$35	$35	$35
$35	$35	$35	$35
$35	$35	$35	$35
$35	$35	$35	
$35	$35	$35	

E-Power: 17 (work)/$630(18-dues)
E-Plus: 17 (work)/$2,040(contribute)

Chapter A Year 3

$35	$35	$35	$35	$35
$35	$35	$35	$35	$35
$35	$35	$35	$35	$35
$35	$35	$35	$35	$35
$35	$35	$35	$35	$35

E-Power: 23 (work)/$870(25-dues)
E-Plus: 23 (work)/$2,760(contribute)

OR

Chapter A

$35	$35	$35	$35	$35
$35	$35	$35	$35	$35
$35	$35	$35	$35	$35
$35	$35	$35	$35	$35
$35	$35	$35	$35	$35

E-Power: 23 (work)/$870(25-dues)
E-Plus: 23 (work)/$2,760(contribute)

Chapter B

$35	$35	$35	$35	$35	$35
$35	$35	$35	$35	$35	$35
$35	$35	$35	$35	$35	$35
$35	$35	$35	$35	$35	$35
$35	$35	$35	$35	$35	$35

E-Power: 27 (work)/$1,050(30-dues)
E-Plus: 27 (work)/$3,240(contribute)

Chapter C

$35	$35	$35	$35	$35	$35
$35	$35	$35	$35	$35	$35
$35	$35	$35	$35	$35	$35
$35	$35	$35	$35	$35	$35
$35	$35	$35	$35	$35	$35

E-Power: 34 (work)/$1,296(36-dues)
E-Plus: 34 (work)/$4,080(contribute)

Again, this depiction of reduced dues is to strengthen a Brother's economic power in the Chapter. With the addition of the Chapter and based on an ideal budget, a Brother might be able to afford to maintain membership in both the Lodge and the Chapter. With this economic power and the start of a Chapter, you allow Brothers to voluntarily purchase an item, make an item, or liberally donate money to causes as their individual financial situations allow. By allowing a Brother to give as his financial situation allows, you are giving a Brother full latitude to support the Lodge and Chapter without forcing him to pay an arbitrary amount that he may not be able to afford. A Brother can continue to afford to be in the room, to participate, and you can get him to serve and support any other cause in the Lodge and Chapter. He does not have to be resentful or conflicted by not being able to afford to be a part of both organizations. This also provides greater viability for the establishment and sustainment of a Royal Select Council. The ability to sustain one or two Councils greatly improves with the consistently positive growth of one or more Lodges and Chapters.

We can see this illustrated in a different way if a Lodge and Chapter are both aligned and are addressing growth and retention issues or avoiding common pitfalls and challenges and fostering a positive community-facing and membership experience. Consider where affordability is a retention strategy, but the Lodge and Chapter still face common issues with attrition due to death, age and mobility, transfers, lack of interest, dissatisfaction, and lack of participation. Here, as with the Lodge and Chapter, you may have Brothers who choose to still pay their dues to the Council while participating more in Lodge activities. And they continue to pay dues to support all three organizations because it is affordable. Though the organizations may experience a slight degradation in participating force, a continued adjustment on behalf of the Lodge and Chapter to improve the quality of community-facing and membership activities, while making membership affordable, will ensure the viability and sustainment of the York Rite.

Lodge A

$35	$35	$35	$35	$35
$35	$35	$35	$35	$35
$35	$35	$35	$35	$35
$35	$35	$35	$35	$35
$35	$35	$35	$35	$35
		$35	$35	$35
$35	$35	$35	$35	$35

E-Power: 31 (work)/$1,188(33-dues)
E-Plus: 31 (work)/$3,480(contribute)

Lodge B

$35	$35	$35	$35	$35	$35
$35	$35	$35	$35	$35	$35
$35	$35	$35	$35	$35	$35
$35	$35	$35	$35	$35	$35
$35	$35	$35	$35	$35	$35
$35		$35	$35	$35	$35
$35	$35	$35	$35	$35	$35

E-Power: 38 (work)/$1,404(41-dues)
E-Plus: 37 (work)/$4,440(contribute)

Lodge C

$35	$35	$35	$35	$35	$35
$35	$35	$35	$35	$35	$35
$35	$35	$35	$35	$35	$35
$35	$35	$35	$35	$35	$35
$35	$35	$35	$35	$35	$35
$35	$35	$35	$35	$35	$35

E-Power: 34 (work)/$1,296(36-dues)
E-Power: 34 (work)/$4,080(contribute)

Chapter A

$35	$35	$35	$35	$35
$35	$35	$35	$35	$35
$35	$35	$35	$35	$35
$35	$35	$35	$35	$35
$35	$35	$35	$35	$35

E-Power: 24 (work)/$875(25-dues)
E-Plus: 24 (work)/$2,880(contribute)

Chapter B

$35	$35	$35	$35	$35	$35
$35	$35	$35	$35	$35	$35
$35	$35	$35	$35	$35	$35
$35	$35	$35	$35	$35	$35
$35	$35	$35	$35	$35	$35

E-Power: 28 (work)/$1,050(30-dues)
E-Plus: 28 (work)/$3,360(contribute)

Chapter C

$35	$35	$35	$35	$35	$35
$35	$35	$35	$35	$35	$35
$35	$35	$35	$35	$35	$35
$35	$35	$35	$35	$35	$35
$35	$35	$35	$35	$35	$35

E-Power: 35 (work)/$1,260(36-dues)
E-Power: 35 (work)/$4,200(contribute)

The Health of the Chapter. As your Chapter goes through population changes, evaluate the organizational health. Again, as before with the Lodge, with the health of your Chapter, consider the number of members in and the number of members out as a matter of growth/turnover and retention in a given year. Using a growth rate and a retention rate is a good way to measure the health of your organization. This can be useful at any level of the organization, for any one or multiple organizations in a geographical area.

A consistent positive growth rate equal to or greater than 25 percent allows the Lodge and Chapter the ability to support the growth of the York Rite with little impact from the pitfalls of things like misrepresentation and perversion, and community-facing activities. This shows the Lodge and Chapter's capacity to grow the economic power necessary to be able to better serve the community without strain on the membership. A consistent retention rate equal to or greater than 85 percent allows the Lodge and Chapter the ability to support the growth of the York Rite with little impact from community and membership-facing activities. This shows the Lodge and Chapter's capacity to provide a satisfying membership experience and retain economic power. A growth rate of less than 25 percent would make sustainment tough in the long run. A retention rate of less than 75 percent runs counter to the 25 percent growth rate needed to support and sustain growth across the York Rite.

A Council of Royal Select Masons

Because we tend to operate under the same adverse practices, the same pitfalls and challenges of the Lodge and Chapter will fall on the Council. The way in which it operates as an organization in both its community and membership-facing activities will have a bearing on its membership. The Council still has to be concerned with things like misrepresentation and perversion, fraternal politics, membership interests and satisfaction, leadership alignment, and affordability. The Council is one tier from the Lodge, so there is no direct pipeline. Once established, there needs to be a continuous assessment of the Council's economic power, growth and retention rates, and geographical area to constitute the establishment of a Commandery. Again, like the Chapter and the Council, a Commandery can be deemed viable through the support of one or more Lodges, Chapters, and Councils.

The Council's Growth. The growth of the Council depends on the population of the Lodges and Chapters. Like the Lodge and Chapter, the Council has to take care in both its community and membership-facing activities and leadership alignment. The Council will also have its jurisdiction designated by district, region, or province as a sovereign space, but the Council must not operate in a way that is exclusive of the Lodges or Chapters operating in the same space. With the addition of the Council, leadership alignment takes on another layer of meetings, service events, and affordability. There should be growth and recruitment initiatives and objectives particular to the Lodge, Chapter, and Council.

The Lodge and Chapter will provide a population pool of qualified Brothers from which the Council should actively recruit. As with the Lodge, the Council membership should reflect a volume of equal to or greater than 25 percent of the Lodge and Chapter population or the overall population of all Lodges and Chapters. There may be a minimum of nine members required to constitute a Council as well, but this number may also be set to twelve or fifteen. It should be expected that it may take one Chapter some time to grow the membership needed to support the idea of having a Council, while it may not take as long if a Council is to be supported by three Lodges or Chapters.

There has been discussion of how three Lodges might support a Chapter, but a Council might be supported by a combination of one or more of either. Here is an example and illustration of forming a Council with three Lodges and one or three Chapters:

Lodge A (36)

LG	LG	LG	LG	LG	LG
LG	LG	LG	LG	LG	LG
LG	LG	CH	CH	CH	CH
LG	LG	CH	CH	CH	CH
LG	LG	CH	CH	CH	CH
LG	LG	LG	LG	LG	LG

Lodge B (42)

LG	CH	CH	LG	LG	LG	LG
LG	CH	CH	LG	LG	LG	LG
LG	CH	CH	CH	LG	LG	LG
LG	CH	CH	CH	LG	LG	LG
LG	CH	CH	LG	LG	LG	LG
LG	CH	CH	LG	LG	LG	LG

Lodge C (36)

LG	LG	LG	LG	LG	LG
LG	LG	LG	CH	CH	LG
LG	LG	CH	CH	CH	LG
LG	LG	CH	CH	CH	LG
LG	LG	CH	CH	CH	LG
LG	LG	CH	CH	CH	LG

Chapter A Year 1 (15)

CH	CH	CL
CH	CH	CL
CH	CH	CL
CH	CH	CL
CH	CH	CH

25 percent (4) is not enough to warrant a Council.

Chapter A Year 2 (25)

CH	CH	CH	CH	CL
CH	CH	CH	CH	CL
CH	CH	CH	CH	CL
CH	CH	CH	CH	CL
CH	CH	CH	CL	CL

25 percent (6) with a little growth is not enough to warrant a Council.

Chapter A Year 3 (40)

CH	CH	CH	CH	CH	CH	CL	CL
CH	CH	CH	CH	CH	CH	CL	CL
CH	CH	CH	CH	CH	CH	CL	CL
CH	CH	CH	CH	CH	CH	CL	CL
CH	CH	CH	CH	CH	CH	CL	CL

25 percent (10) near minimum is enough to warrant a Council.

OR

Chapter A (30)

CH	CH	CH	CH	CH
CH	CH	CH	CH	CH
CH	CH	CH	CH	CH
CH	CL	CL	CL	CL
CH	CH	CL	CL	CL
CH	CH	CH	CH	CH

Chapter B (36)

CH	CH	CL	CL	CH	CH
CH	CH	CL	CL	CH	CH
CH	CH	CL	CL	CH	CH
CH	CH	CL	CL	CH	CH
CH	CH	CH	CH	CH	CH
CH	CH	CH	CH	CH	CH

Chapter C (30)

CH	CH	CH	CH	CH
CH	CH	CH	CL	CH
CH	CH	CL	CL	CH
CH	CH	CL	CL	CH
CH	CH	CL	CL	CH

Council A (24)

CL	CL	CL	CL
CL	CL	CL	CL
CL	CL	CL	CL
CL	CL	CL	CL
CL	CL	CL	CL
CL	CL	CL	CL

Establish a Council with 25 percent (24) of your overall Chapter population.

A single Chapter may not have the growth needed to constitute a Council. Even where the slightest of growth might provide what appears to be sufficient numbers, use the minimum number needed to constitute the organization first, then have the measure of 25 percent of the Chapter as a buffer. Also consider using a reasonable factor of three to add a greater buffer to pursue a higher-than-needed membership volume to start. The addition of a buffer ensures the Council can sustain its membership through the first three years or so until it can start to realize consistent positive growth.

Due to its indirect distance from the Lodge where it fits in the York Rite hierarchy, growth in the Council will take a little longer than that of the Chapter. Where two or more Chapters form a pipeline to one Council, the establishment and growth may not be as challenging as that encountered by one Chapter, one pipeline. The idea of three Chapters and three pipelines to one Council does provide a third level of complexity for alignment.

Consider your internal, Council, and fraternity-facing aspect, your Council's administration and business environment. Your initial engagements with a potential Companion are a first and lasting impression. It is still equally important to have a well-rehearsed and proficient degree team. Like the Lodge and Chapter, the work of the Council and the presence of the Council set the beginnings of what is to come for membership retention. In the Council you will have to work harder to keep members engaged and keep their interests. Develop a sense of cooperation and alignment with the Lodge and Chapter to ensure the pipeline from the Chapter is clear of conflict and competing interests.

The Council's Membership Retention. Consider all the before-mentioned suggestions for retention provided for the Lodge and the Chapter. Membership retention in the Council will still require attention to a Brother's membership experience, possibly to a greater extent. By the time a Brother arrives at the Council, he has increased his knowledge in the administrative and business matters of the fraternity. So, the atmosphere in the Council still needs to be one of inclusion, free and open discussion, sound business practices, and transparency. The decision making is still with the members of the Council. An environment in the Council where the well-being of your members and the operating health of the Council are well-considered is positive. You still have to assess a Companion's preparedness to lead the Council to ensure adverse practices do not contribute to a loss in membership.

The Council has to work twice as hard to keep the members it has. Remember, the Council is competing with the environments established in the Chapter and the Lodge. Time and space and affordability are even more of a factor for growth and retention at the Council level. A Brother will decide if his time and money are worth the experience here, and the Council could lose him back to the Chapter and/or the Lodge.

The Importance of Leadership Alignment. With the idea of the Council added as a third tier, we must revisit leadership alignment. This requires collective teamwork, cohesion, collaboration, cooperation, assistance, and a sense of shared interest and responsibility across the Lodge, Chapter, and Council. The two driving factors for alignment, again, are time and money. Because we can establish organizations with various different combinations of structures, the approach to alignment should be based on the complexity of structure. A one-to-one-to-one (1 Lodge, 1 Chapter, 1 Council) structure is not as complex as it might be for a three-to-two-to-one (3 Lodges, 2 Chapters, 1 Council) structure.

Lodge A

LG	LG	LG
LG	LG	LG
LG	LG	LG

Lodge B

LG	LG	LG
LG	LG	LG
LG	LG	LG

Lodge C

LG	LG	LG
LG	LG	LG
LG	LG	LG

Council A

CL	CL	CL
CL	CL	CL
CL	CL	CL
CL	CL	CL

Chapter A

CH	CH	CH	CH
CH	CH	CH	CH
CH	CH	CH	CH

Chapter B

CH	CH	CH	CH
CH	CH	CH	CH
CH	CH	CH	CH

What further complicates alignment with the addition of an organization at any tier of the York Rite is our natural course to take the path of least resistance. We will first look for the date and time slot that is not already taken by another organization to avoid meeting at the same time. Then, with a new or different organization, we look to do new or different things. Time might further be a conflict for any Brother who is a member of a Lodge, a Chapter, and the newly constituted Council. We may look at this from the point of view of the members of each organization, who have a right to do whatever they want, but the members across the organizations are all the same people. Because of the way we are accustomed to doing things, we decide against our own interests. So, in our natural course, we shape our own chaos.

Every single meeting and event accounts for time away from our families. Often to our own detriment, we want to attend everything. We might find ourselves away every Saturday because that is how we scheduled our meetings. Other times where the Lodge has two meetings, unless that Lodge is conducting a large volume of business every two weeks, that second meeting is a waste of our time. We never think to cut the number of meetings, co-sponsor, or do joint activities.

The Economic Power of the Council. We will revisit the idea of economic power because we are susceptible to enacting the same practice of setting high amounts for Council dues while ignoring the long-term drag on the rest of the organization. Again, a Council of men as labor and resources serves the community to bring about positive social change in the name of Freemasonry. As the Council goes through changes and makes decisions, there needs to be consideration given to this operating aspect of the organization to ensure it can continue to grow to survive beyond the first three years or combat stagnation or lack of growth. The economic power of the Council is based on a Brother's ability to participate and contribute liberally to the Council. Here is an illustration of the potential in economic power of a Council with our usual application of dues structure:

Council A Year 1

$100	$100	$100
$100	$100	$100
$100	$100	$100
$100	$100	$100
$100	$100	$100

E-Power: 15 (available to work)
E-Power: 15 (pay dues)/$1,500

Council A Year 2

$100	$100	$100
$100	$100	$100
$100		$100
$100		
$100	$100	$100

E-Power: 11 (available to work)
E-Power: 12 (pay dues)/$1,200

Council A Year 3

$100	$100	$100	$100
$100	$100	$100	$100
$100		$100	$100
$100			
$100			

E-Power: 12 (available to work)
E-Power: 12 (pay dues)/$1,200

The economic power of the Council will also be limited to those Companions who can afford to pay dues. Like before, these same Companions may not be able to afford to do anything more for the Council. From year to year, the Council will endure some kind of change. In this illustration, a Council might begin with fifteen members in Year 1 and may not bring in any members in Year 1. In Year 2, you have four who leave to participate only in the Lodge and Chapter, but two Companions still pay dues. Later, in Year 3, the Council brings in three new members while losing an additional Companion, who only wants to participate in the Chapter, with five nonpaying members. The Council will continue to face the same challenges, with the added elements of competing environments in the Lodge and Chapter and affordability.

When one or more Chapters or Lodges are challenged with growth and retention, and issues of affordability, this will greatly impact the Council. As stated before, the growth and retention of the overall population of the Council will provide some sense of viability to establish a Commandery, but affordability and other common issues will likely continue to plague the Lodges and Chapters and spread to the Council. This illustration revisits high dues and attrition in the Lodge and Chapter, and how a continuation of this will impact the Council.

Lodge A

$170	$170	$170	$170
$170	$170	$170	$170
$170	$170	$170	$170
$170	$170		
$170	$170		

E-Power: 13 (available to work)
E-Power: 16 (pay dues)/$2,720
E-Plus: None

Lodge B

$170	$170	$170		$170
$170	$170	$170		$170
$170	$170			$170
$170	$170			$170
$170	$170			$170

E-Power: 13 (available to work)
E-Power: 17 (pay dues)/$2,890

Lodge C

$170	$170		$170
$170			$170
$170		$170	$170
$170			$170
$170	$170		$170

E-Power: 8 (available to work)
E-Power: 13 (pay dues)/$2,210

Chapter A

$100	$100	$100
$100	$100	
$100		
$100	$100	$100

E-Power: 9 (available to work)
E-Power: 9 (pay dues)/$900
E-Plus: None

Chapter B

$100		$100
	$100	
	$100	$100
$100		$100
$100	$100	

E-Power: 8 (available to work)
E-Power: 9 (pay dues)/$900

Chapter C

	$100	$100	$100
	$100	$100	$100
$100	$100	$100	$100
$100			$100
			$100

E-Power: 10 (available to work)
E-Power: 13 (pay dues)/$1,300

Council A Year 1

$100	$100	$100
$100	$100	$100
$100	$100	$100
$100	$100	$100
$100	$100	$100

E-Power: 15 (available to work)
E-Power: 15 (pay dues)/$1,500
E-Plus: None

Council A Year 2

$100	$100	$100
$100	$100	$100
$100		$100
$100		
$100	$100	$100

E-Power: 11 (available to work)
E-Power: 17 (pay dues)/$1,700

Council A Year 3

$100	$100	$100
$100	$100	$100
$100	$100	$100
$100		
$100		

E-Power: 8 (available to work)
E-Power: 13 (pay dues)/$1,300

Your Council will endure some kind of change. The Council might miss out on some qualified Brothers who cannot continue to afford the high cost of dues. In this illustration, your Council might begin with fifteen members in Year 1. Being preceded by struggling Lodges and Chapters, you may not bring in any new members through Year 3 and then lose Companions back to either the Lodge, Chapter, or both. Still, you will have Companions who can either no longer participate because of time conflicts but still pay their dues ($170 + $100 + $100 = $370), or who cannot afford to pay dues for all three organizations. Here is how a Council might struggle from inception with the cascading effect of struggling Lodges and/or struggling Chapters. The Council does not have to continue to set high dues. In the same vein, issues of affordability, lack of interest, dissatisfaction, and lack of participation can be addressed at the Lodge and Chapter levels, but this is where operating pitfalls, leadership alignment, and affordability strategy need to be considered.

Let's look at possibilities if the Lodges and Chapters are addressing growth and retention issues or avoiding common pitfalls and challenges and fostering a positive community-facing and membership experience. Consider affordability for the Council, but the Lodge and Chapter still face common issues with attrition due to death, age and mobility, transfers, lack of interest, dissatisfaction, and lack of participation. It is not uncommon for Brothers to decide on some degree of participation due to conflicts created across each of the organizations. This is, again, why alignment is important. You may have Brothers and Companions who choose to still pay their dues to the Lodge and Chapter while participating more in, say, the Council. And they continue to support the Lodge, Chapter, and Council by paying dues because it is affordable to do so.

Leading Masonic Organizations

Council A Year 1

$35	$35	$35
$35	$35	$35
$35	$35	$35
$35	$35	$35
$35	$35	$35

E-Power: 15 (work)/$525 (15-dues)
E-Plus: 15 (work)/$1,800 (contribute)

Council A Year 2

$35	$35	$35	$35	$35
$35	$35	$35	$35	$35
$35	$35	$35	$35	$35
$35	$35	$35	$35	$35
$35	$35	$35	$35	$35

E-Power: 23 (work)/$875 (25-dues)
E-Plus: 23 (work)/$2,760 (contribute)

Council A Year 3

$35	$35	$35	$35	$35	$35
$35	$35	$35	$35	$35	$35
$35	$35	$35	$35	$35	$35
$35	$35	$35	$35	$35	$35
$35	$35	$35	$35	$35	$35

E-Power: 27 (work)/$1,050 (30-dues)
E-Plus: 27 (work)/$3,240 (contribute)

OR

Council A

$35	$35	$35	$35	$35
$35	$35	$35	$35	$35
$35	$35	$35	$35	$35
$35	$35	**$35**	$35	$35
$35	$35	$35	$35	$35

E-Power: 24 (work)/$875 (25-dues)
E-Plus: 24 (work)/$2,880 (contribute)

Council B

$35	$35	$35	$35	$35	$35
$35	$35	$35	$35	$35	$35
$35	$35	**$35**	$35	**$35**	$35
$35	**$35**	$35	$35	$35	$35
$35	$35	$35	$35	$35	$35

E-Power: 27 (work)/$1,050 (30-dues)
E-Plus: 27 (work)/$3,240 (contribute)

Council C

$35	$35	$35	$35	$35	$35
$35	$35	$35	$35	$35	$35
$35	$35	**$35**	$35	$35	$35
$35	**$35**	**$35**	$35	$35	$35
$35	$35	$35	$35	$35	$35

E-Power: 27 (work)/$1,050 (30-dues)
E-Plus: 27 (work)/$3,240 (contribute)

The reduction in dues is to continue to strengthen a Brother's economic power in the Lodge, Chapter, and now, the Council. A Brother might afford to maintain membership in all three organizations. Again, with greater economic power, you are allowing a Brother to give as his financial situation allows; you are giving a Brother full latitude to support the Lodge, Chapter, and Council, without forcing him to pay an arbitrary amount that he may not be able to afford. A Brother can continue to afford to be in the room, to participate, and you can get him to serve and support any cause in the Lodge, Chapter, and Council. His greatest challenge is no longer affordability per se, but finding the time to support the activities of the Council, Chapter, and Lodge. As with the requisite consideration for the Chapter and Council, this also provides greater viability for the establishment and sustainment of a Commandery.

The ability to sustain one or two Commanderys greatly improves with the consistently positive growth of one or more Lodges, Chapters, and Councils. The following is a depiction of how things might look when Lodges, Chapters, and Councils are aligned and addressing common pitfalls and issues, while still facing challenges related to attrition:

Lodge A

$35	$35	$35	$35	$35
$35	$35	$35	$35	$35
$35	$35	$35	$35	$35
$35	$35	$35	$35	$35
$35	$35	$35	$35	$35
		$35	$35	$35
$35	$35	$35	$35	$35

E-Power: 31 (work)/$1,155 (33-dues)
E-Plus: 31 (work)/$3,720 (contribute)

Lodge B

$35	$35	$35	$35	$35	$35
$35	$35	$35	$35	$35	$35
$35	$35	$35	$35	$35	$35
$35	$35	$35	$35	$35	$35
$35	$35	$35	$35	$35	$35
$35		$35	$35	$35	$35
$35	$35	$35	$35	$35	$35

E-Power: 38 (work)/$1,435 (41-dues)
E-Plus: 38 (work)/$4,560 (contribute)

Lodge C

$35	$35	$35	$35	$35	$35
$35	$35	$35	$35	$35	$35
$35	$35	$35	$35	$35	$35
$35	$35	$35	$35	$35	$35
$35	$35	$35	$35	$35	$35
$35	$35	$35	$35	$35	$35
$35	$35			$35	$35

E-Power: 38 (work)/$1,400 (40-dues)
E-Plus: 38 (work)/$4,560 (contribute)

Chapter A

$35	$35	$35	$35	$35
$35	$35	$35	$35	$35
$35	$35	$35	$35	$35
$35	$35	$35	$35	$35
$35	$35	$35	$35	$35

E-Power: 24 (work)/$1,225 (35-dues)
E-Plus: 24 (work)/$2,880 (contribute)

Chapter B

$35	$35	$35	$35	$35	$35
$35	$35	$35	$35	$35	$35
$35	$35	$35	$35	$35	$35
$35	$35	$35	$35	$35	$35
$35	$35	$35	$35	$35	$35

E-Power: 28 (work)/$1,050 (30-dues)
E-Plus: 28 (work)/$3,360 (contribute)

Chapter C

$35	$35	$35	$35	$35	$35
$35	$35	$35	$35	$35	$35
$35	$35	$35	$35	$35	$35
$35	$35	$35	$35	$35	$35
$35	$35	$35	$35	$35	$35

E-Power: 29 (work)/$1,050 (30-dues)
E-Plus: 29 (work)/$3,480 (contribute)

Council A Year 1

$35	$35	$35
$35	$35	$35
$35	$35	$35
$35	$35	$35
$35	$35	$35

E-Power: 15 (work)/$5255 (15-dues)
E-Plus: 15 (work)/$1,800 (contribute)

Council A Year 2

$35	$35	$35	$35	$35
$35	$35	$35	$35	$35
$35	$35	$35	$35	$35
$35	$35	$35	$35	$35
$35	$35	$35	$35	$35

E-Power: 23 (work)/$874 (25-dues)
E-Plus: 23 (work)/$2,760 (contribute)

Council A Year 3

$35	$35	$35	$35	$35	$35
$35	$35	$35	$35	$35	$35
$35	$35	$35	$35	$35	$35
$35	$35	$35	$35	$35	$35
$35	$35	$35	$35	$35	$35

E-Power: 27 (work)/$1,050 (30-dues)
E-Plus: 27 (work)/$3,240 (contribute)

The Health of the Council. The health of the Council is equally important as that of the Lodges and Chapters. Though the Council serves as a middle-tier with the Chapter, it is a step removed from the Lodge, and therefore growth may take a little longer, and retention may be a little tougher. It is important that new and existing Councils assess the growth and retention rates of their organization to capture some idea of the health of the organization. A 25 percent growth rate and an 85 percent retention rate are also markers of good health for the Council. With the lag in pipeline between the Lodge and Council and dependency on the Chapter, growth rates for the Council may be lower than desired from time to time. In times of slow growth, throughout the Chapter more efforts should be on achieving higher retention rates. The Council needs to be watchful and prepared to make adjustments to improve its alignment with the Chapter and its overall membership experience for the growth and sustainment of the York Rite.

A Commandery of Knights Templar

The Commandery is the final organization of the York Rite. It rounds out the fourth tier, and the position of the Commandery puts it at an even greater disadvantage in one regard while implying advantages in some other ways. The Commandery still has to be mindful of how it operates as an organization in both its community and membership-facing activities. It will not be immune from misrepresentation and perversion, fraternal politics, membership interests and satisfaction, training and development, leadership development and alignment, and affordability. Because it completes the York Rite, the existence of the Commandery is just as equally important as the Lodge.

The Commandery's Growth. In terms of growth, the Commandery is waiting on everyone in the other organizations to qualify themselves to be worthy. The Commandery will likely be supported by a host of Lodges, Chapters, and Councils in its district, region, or province. Like the addition of other tiers, the Commandery adds a layer of meetings, service events, and affordability to leadership alignment woes. Due to the proximity of the Commandery to the Lodge, growth initiatives and objectives should be deliberate in producing a pool of Brothers and Companions qualified for membership to the Commandery.

Like the others, the Commandery membership should reflect a volume of equal to or greater than 25 percent of the Lodges' population or the overall population of all Lodges. There may be a minimum of nine members required to constitute a Commandery, but this number may also be set to twelve or fifteen. It should be expected that it may take one Council some time to grow the membership needed to support the idea of having a Commandery, while it may not take as long if a Commandery is to be supported by three Chapters and Councils. As with other examples, here is an illustration of forming a Commandery with one or more Councils:

Council A Year 1 (15)

CL	CL	CM
CL	CL	CM
CL	CL	CM
CL	CL	CM
CL	CL	CL

25 percent (4) is not enough to warrant a Commandery.

Council A Year 2 (25)

CL	CL	CL	CL	CM
CL	CL	CL	CL	CM
CL	CL	CL	CL	CM
CL	CL	CL	CL	CM
CL	CL	CL	$35	CM

25 percent (6) with a little growth is not enough to warrant a Commandery.

Council A Year 3 (40)

CL	CL	CL	CL	CL	CL	CM	CM
CL	CL	CL	CL	CL	CL	CM	CM
CL	CL	CL	CL	CL	CL	CM	CM
CL	CL	CL	CL	CL	CL	CM	CM
CL	CL	CL	CL	CL	CL	CM	CM

25 percent (10) near minimum is enough to warrant a Commandery.

OR

Council A (30)

CL	CL	CL	CL	CL
CL	CL	CL	CL	CL
CL	CL	CL	CL	CL
CL	CM	CM	CM	CM
CL	CL	CM	CM	CM
CL	CL	CL	CL	CL

Council B (36)

CL	CL	CM	CM	CL	CL
CL	CL	CM	CM	CL	CL
CL	CL	CM	CM	CL	CL
CL	CL	CM	CM	CL	CL
CL	CL	CL	CL	CL	CL
CL	CL	CL	CL	CL	CL

Council C (30)

CL	CL	CL	CL	CL
CL	CL	CL	CM	CL
CL	CL	CM	CM	CL
CL	CL	CM	CM	CL
CL	CL	CM	CM	CL

Commandery A (24)

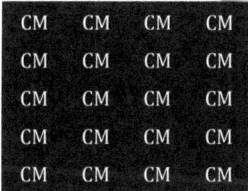

Establish a Commandery with 25 percent (24) of your overall Council population.

As demonstrated before, a single Council may not have the growth needed to constitute a Commandery, or it may take a while. Continuing the use of the number required to constitute a Commandery, adding a buffer of sorts helps establish a comfort level for membership. This should get the Commandery through its first two years should it encounter growth challenges elsewhere in the York Rite. In considering a rule of three again, three Chapters forming a pipeline to one or more Councils should be sufficient to aid growth for the Commandery. The Commandery provides an additional level of complexity to alignment, but it is equally as important to the York Rite as the Lodge. Where the Lodge is the beginning and the Commandery is the end, we cannot start the York Rite without the Lodge, nor can we complete the York Rite without the Commandery.

The Commandery still has to be concerned with its internal administration and business environment. By the time a Brother arrives at the Commandery, there should have been enough experiences of success across the York Rite that Brothers have a keen understanding of fraternity business. Just as with the care and consideration given to a candidate in the Lodge, a well-rehearsed and proficient degree team will have a lasting impression on a Companion. Like everywhere else, this sets the beginnings of what is to come for the Commandery's membership retention. At this point, competing interests can be overwhelming, so cooperation and alignment with the Lodges, Chapters, and Councils may prove to be challenging, but it is necessary.

The Commandery's Membership Retention. The Commandery is competing with the environments of the Council, Chapter, and Lodge. So, the Commandery has to figure out how to keep the members it has. You will still need to be watchful of a Brother's preparedness to lead the Commandery to ensure adverse practices do not contribute to a loss in membership. If the atmosphere in the Councils, Chapters, and Lodges is one of inclusion, free and open discussion, sound business practices, and transparency, then the Companions will likely bring that same atmosphere to the Commandery. This is what you should hope for. The first impression of a Companion will go a long way, so do not neglect the responsibility of putting forward the business in the organization's administration and a proficient degree team. The competition here is not true in nature; it's just that a Brother will decide if his time and money are worth the experience in the Commandery, and the Commandery could lose him back to the Council, Chapter, and/or the Lodge.

The Importance of Leadership Alignment. At the final and last tier of the York Rite, the Commandery will come into an existing operating space already crowded by Councils, Chapters, and Lodges. With the York Rite complete, leadership alignment as a collective is in the name *York Rite*. We are accustomed to often excluding the Lodge because of its exclusive existence. It has become acceptable practice to refer to the York Rite as just the Chapter, Council, and Commandery. Once the three are grouped together from an operational perspective, it seems easier to align among two instead of four (Lodge and then Chapter-Council-Commandery together). Though we know the York Rite includes all four, the later discussion of ease of alignment includes a consideration for the three being grouped.

Because it's one of those customary practices, the structure for the York Rite can shape out into a variety of ways. This one is with multiple Lodges, Chapters, and Councils to support a Commander. Whether it is a one-to-one structure, or three-to-two to two-to-one, every structure provides a degree of complexity with alignment. No matter the structure, it is most important that the York Rite operates as one organization.

Lodge A

LG	LG	LG
LG	LG	LG
LG	LG	LG

Lodge B

LG	LG	LG
LG	LG	LG
LG	LG	LG

Lodge C

LG	LG	LG
LG	LG	LG
LG	LG	LG

Commandery A

CM	CM	CM
CM	CM	CM
CM	CM	CM
CM	CM	CM

Chapter A

CH	CH	CH
CH	CH	CH
CH	CH	CH

Chapter B

CH	CH	CH
CH	CH	CH
CH	CH	CH

Chapter C

CH	CH	CH
CH	CH	CH
CH	CH	CH

Council A

CL	CL	CL
CL	CL	CL
CL	CL	CL

Council B

CL	CL	CL
CL	CL	CL
CL	CL	CL

Organize and align for the best result. The existing Councils, Chapters, and Lodges will have established an operating space. Since you are the same members represented across the York Rite, approach alignment in a way that is beneficial to the members of the Commandery. Limit your meetings to the minimum number of required meetings. Avoid creating any net new events and look to co-sponsor and conduct joint events with other organizations across the York Rite. It is not a bad idea, and is almost an expected practice, to conduct York Rite–named events and consider a York Rite meeting day. This does not necessarily exclude the Lodge.

This is what cooperation and collaboration might look like in alignment. Say twenty Brothers from the Lodge(s) volunteered at the food bank every year on the third Saturday in September, and these Brothers are also members of the Chapter, Council, and/or Commandery. Then, on September 16, 2018, the Lodge(s), Chapter(s), Council(s), and Commandery also volunteered at the food bank on September 16, 2018. In another way, the Lodge(s) already conduct a toy drive and a voter registration event every year. Now, the Lodge and Chapter headline and partner to sponsor the toy drive, while the Council and Commandery headline and partner to sponsor the voter registration event, even though it originated with the Lodge. You are not necessarily creating any net new events, just leveraging the work already being done.

Typically, if your Chapter, Council, and Commandery can meet on the same Saturday (and the Lodge) one after the other, this could be of great benefit. This situation provides that Brothers are away from home for only one Saturday out of the month, which is a lot better than the scatter of four meetings into four separate days out of the month. The meetings alone become forty-eight events a year. But on one Saturday, forty-eight meetings become twelve events, or thirty-six meetings (Chapter at 9:00 a.m., Council at 11:00 a.m., Commandery at 1:00 p.m.) become twelve events. All of the members are in one place and present to conduct the business of the organization. And the business reflected in your minutes should be very similar because you should not be creating a lot of different service events just because the organizations' names are different.

If you are the same people represented in the same organizations, doing the same work, do not overtax yourselves by creating more stuff to do. Leverage what the Lodge already has established in its trestle board, and maybe add one event specific to the Chapter, Council, or Commandery, nothing more.

The Economic Power of the Commandery. By now, we understand the point of economic power. This will be limited to a Brother's ability to pay dues, participate in the work of the Commandery, and give liberally to the Commandery. However, if we continue the same practice of setting high dues ($170 Lodge, $100 Chapter, $100 Council, $100 Commandery = $470), the Brothers are likely not to come to the Commandery because they cannot afford it. It is counterproductive to continue this practice, even if the other dues remain high. The first two years may be challenging for the Commandery. Even if there are no growth- and retention-related issues across the York Rite, it may still take time for the Commandery to build its economic power if qualified Brothers are not willing to or cannot afford to petition. So, if there are visible growth issues at the Council, this should be an alarm to the Chapter and the Commandery.

The Commandery, too, will endure some kind of change over time. In this illustration, your Commandery might begin with fifteen members in Year 1. Even if the Lodges and Chapters are not struggling, the Commandery may be able to bring in new members in Year 2 if qualified Brothers are willing to petition, and then may lose a Companion back to the Lodge. Conflicts and competing interests will still influence a Brother's level of participation in Commandery work, but Brothers are likely to continue to keep their dues current in all organizations because it is affordable to do so.

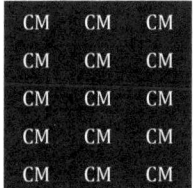

Commandery A Year 1

Commandery A Year 2

Commandery A Year 3

The Health of the Commander and Viability for the York Rite. The health of the Commandery is equally important as that of the Lodge. Being a tier or two removed from the Lodge, like the Council, growth may take a little longer and retention may be a little tougher. However, for this reason, it may serve the Commandery best to focus on higher retention and maintain its numbers. A 25 percent growth rate may not be as easily attainable as, say, an 85 percent retention rate. The Commandery will greatly depend on the Lodge, Chapter, and Council to all have things in order, so lower-than-desired growth should be expected from time to time. The Commandery, too, needs to be watchful and prepared to make adjustments, and willing to do something different to improve its alignment with the other organizations and its overall membership experience for the growth and sustainment and viability of the York Rite.

Here is a structural design of the York Rite carried throughout this book, whereby three Lodges, Chapters, and Councils support a Commandery to round out the York Rite. This can be done the same with one Lodge to one Chapter to one Council and to one Commandery. The idea of three makes the effort of growth and sustainment somewhat easier once the York Rite is established. It will require continuous assessment of the overall economic power and health of each organization to gather a sense of viability for the next organization.

Lodge A (36)

LG	LG	LG	LG	LG	LG
LG	LG	LG	LG	LG	LG
LG	CH	CH	CH	CH	CH
LG	CH	CH	CH	CH	CH
LG	CH	CH	CH	CH	CH
LG	LG	LG	LG	LG	LG

Lodge B (42)

LG	CH	CH	LG	LG	LG	LG
LG	CH	CH	CH	CH	LG	LG
LG	CH	CH	CH	CH	LG	LG
LG	CH	CH	CH	CH	LG	LG
LG	CH	CH	CH	CH	LG	LG
LG	CH	CH	LG	LG	LG	LG

Lodge C (36)

LG	LG	LG	LG	LG	LG
LG	LG	LG	CH	CH	LG
LG	LG	CH	CH	CH	LG
LG	CH	CH	CH	CH	LG
LG	CH	CH	CH	CH	LG
LG	CH	CH	CH	CH	LG

Chapter A (30)

CH	CH	CH	CH	CH
CH	CH	CH	CH	CH
CH	CH	CL	CL	CL
CH	CL	CL	CL	CL
CH	CH	CL	CL	CL
CH	CH	CH	CH	CH

Chapter B (36)

CH	CL	CL	CL	CH	CH
CH	CL	CL	CL	CH	CH
CH	CL	CL	CL	CH	CH
CH	CL	CL	CL	CH	CH
CH	CL	CL	CH	CH	CH
CH	CL	CL	CH	CH	CH

Chapter C (30)

CH	CH	CH	CH	CH
CH	CL	CL	CL	CH
CH	CL	CL	CL	CH
CH	CL	CL	CL	CH
CH	CL	CL	CL	CH

Council A (30)

CL	CL	CL	CL	CL
CL	CL	CL	CL	CL
CL	CL	CL	CL	CL
CL	CM	CM	CM	CM
CL	CM	CM	CM	CM
CL	CL	CL	CL	CL

Council B (36)

CL	CL	CM	CM	CL	CL
CL	CL	CM	CM	CL	CL
CL	CL	CM	CM	CL	CL
CL	CL	CM	CM	CL	CL
CL	CL	CL	CL	CL	CL
CL	CL	CL	CL	CL	CL

Council C (30)

CL	CL	CL	CL	CL
CL	CL	CM	CM	CL
CL	CL	CM	CM	CL
CL	CL	CM	CM	CL
CL	CL	CM	CM	CL

Establish a Commandery with 25 percent (24) of your overall Council population.

Commandery A (24)

CM	CM	CM	CM
CM	CM	CM	CM
CM	CM	CM	CM
CM	CM	CM	CM
CM	CM	CM	CM

To Sustain the York Rite

What is our real purpose for existing, if not to develop in the art and science of Freemasonry and progress toward a better future? A York Rite worth building or turning around is worth sustaining not just for today, but for years to come. The York Rite must move as one unit and operate as one organization. This cannot be overstated.

With complexity brought on by the interdependence of each organization and the need for alignment, the York Rite requires constant care. Any decision to start the York Rite must include consideration for the complete complement of the York Rite. The Lodge has to be prepared to support and sustain the Chapter, and when we decide on the Chapter, we should have already determined how and when the Council and Commandery will come. When our existing organizations suffer from time to time, it is time that necessitates change. There needs to be leadership alignment; deliberate, goal-oriented, get-well planning and execution; and a concerted effort to drive positive future growth and development outcomes for the organization. This may require change and the need to see things in a way that we have never seen, hear things in a way that we have never heard, and do some things in a way that we have never done. We cannot afford to wait until we lose a significant number of members, encounter growth problems, or wait until men die to consider changes necessary to continue the advancement of the fraternity.

Set objective markers to assess the health of your organizations. If your Grand Lodge membership is four thousand Master Masons, then your Grand Chapter, Grand Council, and Grand Commandery membership should each be at a minimum of one thousand members, or 25 percent of the total Grand Lodge population. In any given space where Lodges, Chapters, Councils, and Commanderys are aligned by true district, regional, or provincial integrity, the overall Chapter, Council, and Commandery membership should be 25 percent of the overall Lodge population in that area.

Investigate the business of your Lodges and organize strategic pipelines and initiatives to connect the organizations of the York Rite if necessary. An issue at the Lodge level will have an impact at every other tier of the York Rite, and any issue at the Chapter will directly impact the Council and Commandery. Pay attention to growth and retention rates from year to year. We are likely experiencing signals that there are growth and retention issues present, but assuming the presiding officers and Brothers are doing well. Take direct interest in the business of our organizations, as doing well is often not the case. We have Brothers today who know well what fraternal governance should look like. Many of them are members of non-masonic organizations that conduct business well on a consistent basis. They often have a better understanding as to how business should be conducted in fraternal organizations. How we conduct business in our Lodges is critical factor as to how satisfied Brothers are with their membership experience.

Ensure that our members are trained and educated in matters of the fraternity. We continue to make decisions that are against our best interests as an organization. Not every member admitted is prepared to be a leader and to work and make decisions on behalf of the fraternity, and not every man elected to the chair is prepared to preside, advise, or instruct in matters of the fraternity. We lose many members because members have the wrong ideas about their roles and responsibilities. It is of very adverse consequence when members believe the presiding officer has some type of power and decision-making control over the organization. Too often the member does not know any better, nor does the presiding officer. There is also this egregious trap of making Freemasonry expensive, and then, with a lack of business acumen, we misuse the money, while providing a poor and undesirable membership experience that is not worthwhile.

A lot of discussion here was about an idea of economic power and a degradation of such power with declining membership. Be considerate of a Brother and his family's time. Two meetings a month is wasteful. Brothers are not going to allow the structure of Freemasonry to control or disrupt their lives. They will simply leave. The average active presence within an organization is six to eight members, and we cannot afford to keep perpetuating this proud idea of the faithful few because the faithful few are tired and overtaxed. We need to focus on the whole of a Brother's membership experience and fix why the Brothers are leaving. That may require us to clean up the environment within our organizations. It is going to take some courage to stand against age-old adverse practices and those of us who refuse to change. We have to be willing to do it for the good of the Order.

If we work to retain them, then we don't have to reclaim them. We place a lot of emphasis on and develop campaigns around reclaiming Brothers but fail to provide a decent membership experience while we have them. Many of our organizations need better leadership. We have to do better at how we run organizations in giving more attention to the well-being of our members. We lose members, too, because their expectations are often unfulfilled. We fail to get them engaged and fail to keep their interests. There is a need for the adequate preparedness of our members to be better leaders of the fraternity. We are allowing too many to run our organizations into the ground. Many times, Brothers only hear from the organization when dues are due. We need to get better at maintaining constant contact and giving proof of life. Every Brother on your rolls (active and non-active; nonpayment of dues) should receive some type of monthly wellness report or newsletter from the organization. This helps to keep contact and signify that both the Brother and the organization are alive and well. There are some organizations that do this better than others. With this approach, we do not have to subject ourselves to dry sales calls and insult a Brother by requesting he pay his dues. If we are maintaining genuine, constant, and positive contact with all members, Brothers will reach out and inquire as to how they can help the organization (if not present, they will likely donate money) and even be willing to reinstate their membership status and pay their dues without being asked to do so.

Though Freemasonry is the same everywhere, the cost of membership seems to be drastically different depending on where you are. We have to make membership affordable and worthwhile for our Brothers, especially those who desire to improve themselves and maturate through the different colleges of Freemasonry. We will face attrition through death, age and mobility, and transfers, and should avoid practices that contribute to lack of interest, dissatisfaction, and lack of participation. Base your organizational dues on a budget. Membership dues should be based on the minimum required finances needed to operate the organization. It should not be a made-up number. Again, the explanation of such sounds just as it is, a made-up number. A budget should be a mandatory requirement as it demonstrates sound financial decision making and builds trust. Make your dues amount the minimum required to operate the organization plus a carryover buffer as desired by the membership. We have to consider affordability across the York Rite. The Chapter, Council, and Commandery all have to be aware of Lodge dues as well as dues for their respective organizations. We have to account for the complete economic situation of all members, and put Brothers in the greatest position to be able to give liberally to all organizations.

Offer Brothers an option of life membership and structure it in such a way that might achieve economic benefit for both the Brother and the organization. It is a greater likelihood that the monetary value of life membership to the organization will outlive the member. As an example, the Grand Lodge might offer a life membership of $2,500 and the Lodge $1,000, and in some jurisdictions, that is an equivalent monetary value of fifty years of Grand Lodge dues and twenty years of Lodge dues. In other jurisdictions that may only be equivalent to ten years of Grand Lodge dues and four years of Lodge dues. If your current dues structure is high, a high rate for a thing such as life membership may prove to be a waste of time but should also signal a need for a more affordable structure.

Maybe consider the number of consecutive years as a member of the fraternity (not jurisdiction) without any suspension or lapse of membership as eligibility criteria. Any subsequent suspension or expulsion for misconduct forfeits any existing life membership, and a reinstatement after suspension will restart life membership eligibility criteria. Consider some administrative designation like life member number, lapel pin, and certificate. The following is an example of a life membership structure:

Membership	Grand Lodge-Chapter-Council-Commandery Level	Lodge-Chapter-Council-Commandery Level
< 2 years	$2,500	$2,000
5 years - 10 years	$2,000	$1,750
>10 years	$1,750	$1,500
>20 years and 65 years old	$1,000 Life Member granted	$1,250 Life Member granted
Life Member Demit	$500	$500

This suggested demit, or transfer of life membership, would assume all affiliated jurisdictions would have such a structure and/or recognize the life membership afforded from another jurisdiction. Having a demit fee to transfer life membership to another jurisdiction may be reasonable. Also, focus on an immediate offering for new members as a means to aid retention. Allow these to be achieved exclusive of each other so that a Brother might pursue life membership whenever he is financially able to do so.

The residual benefit to the organization is a consistent uptick in financial resources at both the Grand and Lodge levels, assuming some percentage of Brothers will apply to life membership each year. Brothers will likely retain their membership in a particular jurisdiction for a long time. The security of life membership will also serve as another means to improve the economic power of each organization by which a Brother will continue to give liberally to support the cause of the Lodges, Chapters, Councils, and Commanderys.

Once we have built internal sustainable economic power across the York Rite, we should be able to achieve anything. In the same vein, we should have a greater and more positive external social and economic impact on our communities. To establish and maintain a positive presence and identity. We have to improve our business acumen and structure ways in which our organizations might function as community-servicing business units. To operate in the capacity of a legitimate business organization, we must expand our economic capability and impact. Because our advancement as a fraternity is often limited to the vision and skill of the existing leadership and our lack of courage to change, it is going to take the right men and resources, and a willingness to change in order to achieve greater. We need a greater cause to develop greater men to advance the principal ideas and economic prosperity of the fraternity for the next century, not the next year, to not merely make good men better, but to make good men greater. Time will not allow us to escape this responsibility.

Be someone's positive and inspiring example of Freemasonry.

www.ingramcontent.com/pod-product-compliance
Lightning Source LLC
LaVergne TN
LVHW011848060526
838200LV00054B/4221